M. John Harrison was born in 1945. He published his first story in 1966, and has subsequently published five novels and three collections of stories. After spending ten years climbing and fell-running in Yorkshire, he now lives in London.

By the same author

Viriconium
The Ice Monkey

M. JOHN HARRISON

Climbers

Paladin
An Imprint of Grafton Books
A Division of HarperCollins*Publishers*

Paladin
An Imprint of GraftonBooks
A Division of HarperCollins*Publishers*
77–85 Fulham Palace Road,
Hammersmith, London W6 8JB

Published in Paladin 1991
9 8 7 6 5 4 3 2 1

First published in Great Britain by
Victor Gollancz Ltd 1989

A CIP catalogue record of this book
is available from the British Library

ISBN 0-586-09065-7

Printed in Great Britain by
HarperCollinsManufacturing, Glasgow

Set in Sabon

CONTENTS

PART ONE: WINTER

1	Mirrors	13
2	February: Mental Weather	20
3	Dreams	26
4	Sankey's View	43
5	March, in the End	43

PART TWO: SPRING

6	Masters of the Modern Dance	49
7	Gaz & Sankey	55
8	Getting Out	71
9	Wives	76

PART THREE: SUMMER

10	Escapees	107
11	The Numbers	112
12	Sankey and his Sister	113
13	Keeping Hold	150
14	Victims of Love	152

PART FOUR: FALL

15	A Haunted House	161
16	Soloing	184
17	Death on a Teacake	187
18	December	202
19	Each Small Suicide	205
20	Rock Gardens	218

To the climbers.

"Out of this world we cannot fall."

CHRISTIAN GRABBE

PART ONE

WINTER

I · MIRRORS

I went by bus on a wet day in January to the indoor practice wall of a private sports centre near Leeds. It wasn't very successful. Some of the problems there are quite intimidating, with crux moves well up on them, in damaging situations if you inadvertently let go. The return of my sense of balance had given me secret dreams. I would work the winter out of my muscles. I would dance. But hanging high above the badminton players in that huge cold echoing hall with its stink of sweat and rubber soles, I could only pant and groan and slither back down to the floor.

I sat in the changing rooms afterwards tired out, listening to a repetitive noise which I thought at first must be the sound of children shouting or singing in the swimming pool. Then I realised it was the wind I could hear, rising and falling about the bizarre cantilevered roof of the place.

Two fat boys were washing their hair in the shower. The soap and water made them shine. They stood close together and watched me guardedly as I swilled the gymnast's chalk off my hands so I could look at the cuts underneath, and only began to talk again, about different kinds of lager, when I went to get my clothes. They were just like fat pink seals, backing away from the hand outstretched on the ice. Was I a tourist or a sealer? Either way, shreds of skin hung off three fingers of my left hand where I had jammed and twisted the knuckles into a crack in the concrete wall. I am never quite clear what makes you hang on so hard, even when there is such a short way to fall.

"Prawn cocktail crisps here, nice —" said an oldish woman to her friend, walking up and down in front of the Vendepac machine on the floor above.

"— yes, I've seen them dear, very nice."

They put some coins in, nothing happened, someone showed them what to do. When they had sat down again one of them said, raising her hands to the side of her head, palms inward, and moving them rapidly backwards and forwards as if demonstrating some kind of blinker, "I'm just not straightforward with a mechanical thing. You know."

(As I looked down at the badminton players their white faces had for a moment seemed to be swinging slightly to and fro *above* me.)

The first time I went to that wall was for its official opening. Schofield, who had financed it, looked away when he spoke to you; his venality was deeply impressive. "Enjoy yourselves, lads!" he called. It was free for today, or at least for an hour, so that the climbing press would write him up. "Remember we close at two." Sunday lunch time: thirty or forty of us stood in the hangar-like space, watched disapprovingly by some people who were trying to have a game of tennis, waiting for one of the great working-class climbers of the previous generation to christen it, then bless us as the inheritors of his tradition. Bemused looking and pissed he made one or two jerky moves on the easiest of the problems and went back to the bar. In a low voice Schofield assured him he would never have to pay for his drinks here again. Any time he wanted to come he would be welcome here. They had wheeled out this exhausted man, with his Durham accent and his memories of death by stonefall on the Freney Pillar under the relentless telescopes of European journalists, so that the adventure sports trade could have its last good squeeze of him before he was forgotten; and as we left the hall the tennis players were already lined up to complain.

"Tennis, badminton, squash, a sauna: you can have them all for twelve pounds more on your sub. Don't forget, lads," said Schofield. "Don't forget."

On the way back Normal parked the car on the edge of the moor, to photograph the things which had been dumped there. Normal had a gap in his teeth, he was hyperactive, full of suppressed violence: we had done rock climbs together all over Yorkshire, Lancashire and the Peak District, but nothing yet in Wales or Scotland. He had climbed whenever he could for fifteen years. He had worked on the railways until he fell off a train, then at a Manchester climbing shop, where I met him. On Mondays I signed his unemployment form for him. "I'll never go back now." He ran about on the moor, appearing and disappearing in the rain and cloud. It was wet weather, killing weather. The south west wind, full of sulphur from the badly-managed factories in Stockport and Stalybridge, plastered his thin hair to his face, and his arms and legs stuck out of a long, bulbous waistcoat made of Chinese down. As he hopped about trying to attract my attention he looked like an overgrown insect, a species doomed, unknown, used to a better climate.

"What's out there?" I called, pointing at the slimy ribbon of the Pennine Way, but not quite meaning that.

"Floating Lights Quarry," he said. "Where I died. Come out of that car before I drag you out. Look at this."

He laughed.

Abandoned to the streaming mist, there on the exact watershed of the grouse moor, the exact border between Yorkshire and Greater Manchester, sixteen hundred feet above sea level, giving to these surroundings the rakish, cosy, fake-surrealist air of a cigarette advert, was a three-piece suite out of someone's front room in Hyde: light tan; moquette; sodden. We sat in the armchairs, facing out towards Stand Edge and Floating Lights, across lines of peat hags like black combers rolling in from an infinitely polluted sea. The car-park bobbed gently on the psychic swell. All around its edges at our feet was the site of a murder. The icy pools of the watershed were full of children's clothing. Acrylic dungarees and tracksuits; jumpers and quilted polyester dressing gowns; cotton dresses, slips with a bit of cheap broderie, knickers and little teenage bras. Dozens of plastic dustbin bags had burst and were slowly spewing their contents out on to the moor. Whoever had put them there had preferred bright colours. It looked as if whole families of Asian children had been murdered among the collapsed cardboard boxes, the heaps of industrial sawdust, the used Durex and detached pages of *Spank*. Bare buttocks popped out into the weather. Grey smiles woke up suddenly among the pulp.

We poked about half-heartedly in this stuff for a bit, then went home. We had the photographs, we'd had our free go on Schofield's wall. Who knew what might be buried further out, among the more distant pools beyond the NO TIPPING sign?

"I still can't believe that bloody sofa!"

Some climbers Normal had introduced me to:

Bob Almanac looked like an ageing butcher's boy — tough, stocky, round-faced and cheerful, impeccably polite and very competent. I watched him cleaning a new route at Running Hill Pits, chopping turf and loose rock out of the crack-system with quick deft strokes from the pick of an obsolete ice-hammer. The rain soaked his curly hair as he dangled patiently from the abseil rope, forty feet up in a quarry like a dark slot in the hillside above Diggle. "Anyone else would have gone home an hour ago." Bob had spent his life getting wet in places like this — steep, cold, greasy with a kind of bright green lichen which turns into paste as soon as your hand touches it; places which greet your human energy with resentment — and he didn't seem to notice it any more.

With Almanac you always met his friend David. David was a fireman, whose prematurely white hair gave him a kind but slightly overdressed look, like a professional snooker player. The story was that he once *caught* another climber, who had fallen off while soloing in the quarry above Dovestones Reservoir.

Normal explained, "It's his training. They're trained to instinctively save life, firemen."

David had never said anything to me about it, and whether he was being shy or noncommittal wasn't clear. Dovestones Quarry is loose. Most people would wince away from the shadow of a bird there. David had held out his arms, so there was more to it than training. I observed him discreetly, perhaps hoping things would repeat themselves.

"Too wet to make anything out of this today," conceded Almanac eventually, dropping his hammer in disgust. "Look out below." Mucking around underneath, Normal had got himself showered with earth.

Sankey was frail, lantern-jawed, pale-cheeked. It was as if he had outgrown his strength while he was still a boy, and never grown into it again. He had once been the best climber in the valley. He had a nervous laugh, and a way of saying something ordinary that showed he thought of it as a new and desperate observation. He always wiped his friction boots carefully with a piece of frayed towel before he started to climb. He said: "This is the sort of move you really need chalk for. It seems easier if you put a bit of chalk on your fingers first. Ha ha." It was as if he had invented chalk himself, a long time after the rest of us. We had proper little tailored bags to carry ours in, brightly-coloured, suspended from a bit of nylon tape so our hands were free, bought over the counters of outdoor sports outlets in Sheffield or Manchester. Sankey's chalk bag looked like the inside of a trouser pocket. He carried it in one hand, walking in his stiff way from problem to problem, craning his neck to look up at the difficulties, rubbing his fingertips together thoughtfully.

He lived in a terraced cottage below the local cliffs. I can still imagine him wandering about there rather vaguely at night, or in very bad weather, a mild man full of frustrations, his feet slipping suddenly near the top in the dark wind and rain. In my imagination he looks out of his windows at the stone walls dipping down into a dry valley where the ewes move uneasily in the wind. One of them has a chocolate brown patch, like a saddle slipped to one side, which gives her what he describes to himself as a risky, escaped air, like an old fashioned divorcee. All the walls and rutted tracks seem to meet at the head of the valley, by the flimsy wooden sheds which last year and the year before sheltered the new lambs. The wind has started to knock one of them down. Two or three massive gritstone gateposts lie foundering in the waterlogged mud. The air is saturated. The steep moorside gullies over by Ramsden Clough are still full of damp snow. But Sankey can often sense the end of February now, and feel that dry cold wind which sometimes accompanies it.

In a week, in two, the year will have picked up. Or so he hopes.

When I was a child I always felt as if I was on the verge of discovering something. I thought that if I was patient things would show more of themselves than other people could see. Looking at the colours in an ice cream I caught my breath just as if I had jumped into cold water up to the waist: they had somehow been made fluorescent by the sky at Skegness: it had entered them. After that, appearances had for me a kind of perilous promise, an allure, an immanence. Most children feel like that, I suppose.

My mother took me with her to the cafes and hairdressers of Ilkley, or into Leeds and Bradford for a day's shopping. When I think of Littlewoods, or Marks & Spencer's I remember straight away the clatter of pots, the smell of a match just struck, cigarette smoke, wet woollen coats, voices reduced by the damp warm air to an intimate buzz, out of which you could pick a woman at another table saying, "Enough to realise how miserable things are going to be —" On a wet afternoon in November it sent you to sleep. My mother tore the top off a sachet of sugar and tapped it into the ash-tray. I dabbed my finger in it and looked at her sulkily, wondering where we would have to go next.

There was a tinted plate-glass window the whole length of the place we were in. Through it you could see the car-park in the Bradford rain — long shallow puddles ruffled by the wind, one or two cars parked at careless angles, the back entrance of Smith's or Menzies'. On the inside of the glass was the reflection of the cafe. By an optical accident they were superimposed. It was as if someone had dragged thirty plastic tables out there, and a hundred plastic chairs. The women behind the stainless steel counter wiped their faces with a characteristic gesture in the steam, unconscious of the puddles under their feet.

After I had made this discovery a kind of tranquillity came over me. My mother receded, speaking in charged murmurs. The rattle of cutlery and metal trays reached me only from a great distance as I watched people come into the car-park laughing and hang their coats up on ghostly hooks between the cars. They rubbed their hands and sat down to eat squares of dry battenburg cake and exclaim "Mm," how good it was. There they sat, out in the cold, and smiled at one another. They certainly were a lot more cheerful out there. The wind and rain had no power over them. A man on his own had a letter which he opened and began to read.

"Dear Ted," it said.

Waitresses went to and fro round him in their dark blue nylon overalls, for the most part girls with white legs and flat shoes. Some buttoned the top button of their overalls, some didn't. They carried the trays of food with a thoughtless confidence. When they spoke to one another it was in a language full of ellipses, hints and abrupt changes of subject, in which the concrete things were items and prices. I wanted to go and join them. Their lives, I imagined, like the lives of everyone out there in the car-park, were identical to their way of walking between the tables — a neat, safe, confident movement, a movement without a trace of uncertainty through a less restrictive medium than the one I was forced to inhabit.

"You know what Jackie's like with money," I would say to introduce myself. "No, not big Jackie, Carol's Jackie up at Mason's. She bought herself a new ski-jacket for work, Asda actually, only ten ninety-nine —"

"Well you know *Pam*!" they might reply. Or with a quick shout of laughter, "By the time you've been you-know-where, and bought all those cakes!"

Soon, there was only one car left in the car park, drops of water trembling in the wind on its polished orange bonnet. One of the girls walked up and put her tray down on top of it. She wiped her hands on a·cloth which she took out of the driver's seat without opening the door; and then stood staring ahead as if she had begun to suspect that she was caught up in two worlds. Her image dominated both of them, a patient girl of seventeen with chipped nail varnish and a tired back from sorting cutlery all morning. Suddenly she gave a delighted laugh.

She looked directly out at me and waved.

She stood straight up on tiptoe and beckoned. I could see her mouth open and close to make the words, "Here! Over here!"

She's alive! I thought.

It was a shock. I felt that I was alive, too. I saw in quick succession in the back of my mind: grains of sand from very close up, with the sense that behind me was a broad space of sea, mud, salt and gulls; muddy water in a bucket, like thick smoke turning over and over itself; an ice cream in the sunshine.

"Over here!"

I got up and ran straight into the plate-glass window and was concussed. Someone dropped a tray of cutlery. I heard a peculiar voice, going away from me very fast, say, "What's he done? What's he done now?" Then those first eight or nine years of my life were completed — sealed away from me neatly like the bubble in a spirit level, clearly visible but strange and inaccessible, made of nothing.

There are days when, driving home from some gloomy hole in the hillside near Bolton, you wish the whole world was like this:

White bungalows on a hill, floating against a blue cloud full of rain. A one-track road looping across the moor. Old pop music on the radio. Sore fingertips. Nothing ever again but crags you have never seen before, made of a wonderful new kind of rock.

2 · FEBRUARY: MENTAL WEATHER

Driving through Huddersfield one lunch time we saw Sankey walking slowly along the pavement outside the Yorkshire Bank. He had on a black and white woollen hat and there was an electrical screwdriver in his top pocket. We wound down the windows and waved but he didn't seem to recognise Normal's car. Ten minutes later we passed him again in exactly the same place. When we stopped and shouted he gave a disoriented start, as if he'd just been woken up.

"Oh," he said. "Was that you before? I knew someone was waving but I didn't know it was you. Ha ha."

Had he been into the bank? Or had he been standing there all along, trying to decide who would wave at him at half past twelve in the middle of Huddersfield? Normal was jealous of this vagueness, also of Sankey's habit of wearing a running shoe on one foot and a cheap suede boot on the other.

Before I knew Sankey, Normal always talked enthusiastically about him, urging me, "You must meet him, I'll arrange it."

Sankey, he said, had been climbing for twenty years, and during that time he'd been all over the world, bolting routes in Colorado in the early Sixties, freeing them later in Verdon when the first big push of exploration was going on in that enormous gorge, putting up new ones in Kenya and Norway on crags no one had ever heard of. He had been an acquaintance of Harding, and Layton Kor; he still knew Jill Lawrence. He had once spoken to the legendary technician John Gill, who invented modern climbing on boulders not twenty feet above the ground. All the hardest local problems were of Sankey's invention. Besides, he was mad. And so on. But as soon as I did meet Sankey, Normal began to pretend he had some dark reservation about Sankey's character; and when I said, "I really like Sankey," or, "Sankey's a real lunatic isn't he?" he would reply after a long, thoughtful pause —

"The trouble with Sankey is . . . well, he's a weird guy, that one."

Like calls to like:

Sankey was once on his way to the Lake District along the A65. The weather was hot and the hawthorn blossom, still thick on the roadside hedges, filled his three-wheeler with a smell like drugged sweets. He stopped in a crowded lay-by to get himself a sandwich and when he had finished it decided to sit for ten minutes in the sunshine before he went on. Motorcycles glittered in rows under the trees. Behind the lay-by and a little below it was a wide pool where it flowed under a bridge. Elderly tourists, enchanted by the clean counter and mint-green awning of the Hot Snacks van, wiped bacon fat off their fingers and smiled reminiscently down at the water. A few mentally-retarded teenage boys, on a day out from some institution in Bradford or Rotherham, stood in the queue for cups of tea, clutching their money in hands that seemed too big or not quite the right shape. One of them murmured suddenly,

"I'm a new farm worker on this farm, and this is my dog."

He stood expectantly in front of Sankey.

"I've just got to get to know which fields to spread on. I don't know the buildings but I do know the fields."

He was fifteen or sixteen years of age, dressed in frayed denim shorts and a white singlet, and all his features were very close together in the centre of his face. He carried his teacup with exaggerated care but at an odd angle, as if he didn't quite understand how it worked. His voice was slow and determined.

"I'm new here."

Waiting painfully for Sankey to answer, he screwed up his eyes and tried to read the sign which pointed along the river to "Ruskin's View"; then gave equal attention to the discarded film packs and squashed soft drinks cans on the bank. The light shining through the branches of the trees on to the parked motorcycles seemed to confuse him.

"The dog knows the buildings. He knows the buildings better than me."

"Which farm is that, kid?" Sankey said eventually. "Is it round here?"

But the boy was already walking off, slopping his tea on his white shoes. After he had drunk what remained of it he went into the lavatories, where Sankey found him trying to wash his behind. It was quite clean, but he had his shorts down round his ankles and he was fiddling helplessly with the washbasin taps. "Hey mister!" he appealed. "Do you know if this *works*? I can't get anything out." The lavatory cubicles were full of the smell of hawthorn, strange and lulling in a place like that, which overpowered even the reek of piss.

"I advised him to try pressing," Sankey would later maintain. "He did have a dog though. I saw it. He did have a dog. Ha ha."

Although I had first heard it from him Normal claimed not to believe this story, which was typical of Sankey's gentleness and obliquity. I couldn't understand why. Two months before, it had been, "Sankey does *boulder problems* in his back garden," Sankey could do no wrong, "Oh you must meet Sankey!" Now I had, it was, "Well . . ."

It snowed again before the end of February, poor sleety stuff at first, driven in from the south west on a blustery wind. It settled for an hour or two, then mud like melted brown sugar became visible through it in streaks and feathers on the hillsides; and down in Huddersfield the raw damp air soon turned it transparent and flushed it into the drains. Old men shuffled through the slush to collect their pensions at the Northumberland Street post office, which they left smelling strongly of clothes stored for a long time in a damp place.

"Wind's in thaw quarter," they advised one another.

"Aye, it's in thaw quarter all right. They can't get these causeways cleared of it soon enough for me."

That night in the villages along the edge of the moor, spindrift eddied stealthily in the almost lemon yellow light of the sodium lamps, plastering the walls, furring the doors and padlocks of the coal sheds, piling up in the straw-filled ruts of the farm yards until they were covered up bland and spotless. When Sankey came home from work the wind had changed, thunder growled and banged distantly above it. By the next morning he thought the waterfall in Issue Clough might be frozen hard enough to climb: there were jackets of ice on the electricity supply cables where they drooped slackly from barn to barn, icicles developing along them at intervals like the spines and barbels of pale exotic fish; long lines of icicles hung from the corrugated roof of the milking shed. But by mid-day when, bundled up like a middle-aged farmer's wife in a dirty nylon anorak, he plodded through the village to get coal, his hands hanging in front of him, they had begun to melt. Light poured in over the blackened threshold of the old smokehouse, falling among the eroded beams on to a clutter of broken ladders. A few dry beech leaves blew about in the heap of coal. As he stood there looking in, thunder banged tinnily again over towards Huddersfield.

We went to see him at the weekend and found him drowsily watching *Grandstand*. In the winter the downstairs room of his cottage was always full of fumes from the grate which slowly sent him to sleep. "The young man," said the television, "whose odds have fallen so dramatically from eighty to one to ten to one overnight." Sankey turned it off and gave us instant coffee grey with

23

powdered milk, then hunched his shoulders and folded his arms, bending forward in his chair to gaze into the hearth.

"No drink seems hot enough to me today," he apologised. "Ha ha. Everything seems to go down lukewarm today."

Normal eyed the coffee dubiously.

"As long as it doesn't come up the same way."

"You'd have to be mental," Sankey said, "to go climbing in this."

Nevertheless you can see him on the Polaroid picture I took that afternoon, his bright orange waterproof jacket blowing out behind him like a comic book cape as he stands anxiously looking up at Normal who is stalled out halfway up the crag. The picture deteriorated in some way — perhaps because of the cold — soon after it was taken, chemical changes giving the light a dead green cast and making the rock look black and featureless. Normal seems to be pasted on to it, one arm raised wearily. The snow is the same colour as the sky, and only a row of little outcrops marks the division between the two.

These few buttresses of rough grit, heavily pebbled with quartz and perched like boulders on the skyline, are nice to come to on a summer evening, when the hang gliders lie out on the shallow slopes beneath them in the golden light like exhausted butterflies. The day I took the Polaroid we could hear each separate gust of wind building up miles across the moor before it burst round the arêtes on to us, whipped Normal's rope out into a tight parabolic curve, and whirled off down the valley to strafe the sheep. There was snow packed into all the cracks. When we excavated it we found hard ice underneath, as shiny as solidified Superglue. Our noses ran. The wind pulled the strings of mucus out grotesquely, so that during the instant before they snapped they floated with all the elegance of spider-silk. Our fingers went numb, only to come back to life twenty or thirty feet up, at just the wrong moment, the size of bananas and throbbing with hot-aches.

Eventually Normal had to give in and come down.

"It's no good. I can see what to do but I can't convince myself to do it."

His hands were curled up and broken-looking from the cold. They were bleeding where he had knocked them without knowing on the rock. He pulled his mittens on with his teeth and for a while all three of us huddled beneath a big undercut, where it was a bit warmer. But the wind got in under the lip of it and drove ice into our faces, and soon that became a misery too.

"It's no good."

Normal and Sankey began to pack up the gear, stuffing ropes and harnesses untidily into their rucksacks.

"It seems a bit brighter over there," I said.

"It always seems a bit bloody brighter over there."

I was determined to climb something before I went home.

"Why don't we try the big corner?" I suggested.

I pulled myself up on an awkwardly-sloping ledge, from which I would be able to reach out left for a good flake.

"This looks easy enough. I'll lead it."

Both feet shot from under me as I was trying to stand on it. I lowered myself down again quickly. In this way I went along the base of the outcrop trying climb after climb and never getting any higher than five or six feet above the ground. As usual I left a trail of equipment behind me — a coat thrown over a boulder, a Sticht plate hanging from a bush on a bit of coloured line, a small alloy wedge stuck in a crack. This neglect had become a kind of trade mark. The other climbers had soon got used to it, and now they scoured the crag after me at the end of every day, picking up the things I had forgotten.

"Got your Thermos flask, Mike, got your hat?"

"Better check before we go."

"Is this Mike's glove?"

They egged me on.

3 · DREAMS

Normal's obsession with litter prompted him to bring me photographs his wife had taken of cars and bedsteads and other junk half buried in the sand on the coast between Barmouth and Harlech, where they had recently spent a week in a caravan together. Empty ground stretched away to the caravan site under a heavy sky. Everything — the shingle belt, the frieze of corroded side panels and deformed chrome window frames, the sky itself — had a brownish tinge, as if she had exposed the film in an atmosphere of tars.

"It would have been a really nice place," said Normal. "Apart from that."

His own photographs, of the moquette sofa on the Pennine Way, he had sent to the climbing magazines — there were three of them at the time, two monthly and one bi-monthly, all glossy — but he knew they would be returned. What these magazines wanted, he said, was good colour shots of well-known climbers laybacking on the tips of their fingers above an exotic valley. They weren't interested in anything else. (Ideally, the climber should be soloing, but you could sometimes get away with a rope, as long as it was brand new and pinned elegantly to the rock below him by a few well-spaced runners. Later, I was to hear shots like this called "the pornography of risk", but this seemed a little too apt to be true, or anyway useful.)

While we waited for the better weather at the hinge of March we spent the mornings in a cafe in the town, drinking tea. Out of one window you could see the estate agent's and, across the Huddersfield Road, a shop selling motor parts; out of the other a very fat boy mopping a Volvo under the revetment of local stone, green with lichen and pocked with rusting bolts, at the back of the car park. He paused to stare emptily ahead; reached inside the car suddenly and switched on the radio, which then made sobbing complaining noises like someone in the middle of a petty but damaging confession. The little man at Walker's Men's Wear, with its rattan

26

screens and ailing *Monsteria*, jumped out smiling and waving his arms like a thing on a stick. A bit further down was Riverbank Antiques, a nice oblique building across a bridge. It had once been the abattoir but now they only slaughtered the middle-class tourist.

"Where have all these chairs come from?" the woman who served in the cafe would sometimes say. "I'm sure we've got too many this morning."

Like most climbers Normal was thinking about writing his autobiography.

"I'd call it *Out on the Limits*," he said.

I suspect he hoped I would help him with it.

Dabbling in the sugar bowl with a spoon he said he had once had a dream (this would be part of the book) in which he was jamming his way up an endless perfect crack in some warm part of the world — he thought it might be Yosemite National Park in California. He knew by the very length of the crack that he wasn't on a British cliff. "It was incredible. I was a thousand feet up and still going!" The sun blazed down on his back, the air was as bright as alum solution held up in a glass, he felt as if he had been climbing for days. "But I wasn't tired. Only thirsty." He was dressed in blue nylon shorts and his rock boots were of a new, efficient type with grey suede uppers, made in Spain. The crack was deep and cool, exactly the right size for his hands. "It was just off-vertical."

While he was telling this story two women came in. They had the soft golden-orange fur, turned-up noses, and complex, delicate, transparent little ears of marmosets.

"I wonder how they go on for burials nowadays?" said one of them.

They laughed.

"There's hardly any call for it I suppose. They all get cremated."

They were sisters or cousins; mother and daughter. Normal gave them a long speculative look, and they cast like marmosets quick nervous glances at him as they sat down.

"I felt totally confident," he went on. "It was hard work but every few moves I got a terrific foot-jam in and had a rest." The

27

rock stretched away endlessly on either side of him empty of feature except for the crack, and a pale sandy colour much like freshly-quarried millstone grit. "Imagine! A thousand feet of grit! More! That was how I knew it was a dream. I was on the biggest piece of gritstone the world had ever seen. I knew it would never end, and I would never put a foot wrong. It was the dream climb." There was empty space all round him, it ached away beneath the soles of his feet to the screes a thousand feet below: vibrant, receiving into itself his elation as he moved, only to give it back as a blessing.

"It sounds ideal," I said.

As he was looking into the crack to place his next jam, though, he saw something move. It was another hand, and it was reaching out for his own.

"It wasn't attached to anything. It crept out of some ferns growing in the back of the crack, where there was water sweating out of the rock. It got closer. I knew it lived in the crack: I knew everything about it."

It was this "knowing everything about it" which made him let go and fall, all the way down through the darkening air.

"Pretty desperate, that dream!" he said.

He thought for a minute.

"I hate hand jamming anyway."

Some climbers will tell you that, like hang-glider pilots and steeplejacks, climbers never have falling dreams; others that they always do. Every climber has a version of Normal's dream. In some, that disembodied hand shakes yours, or grips your wrist and *pulls you in*; in others you are placing a key runner when the hand snatches it away into the depths of the rock so that you are left without protection on the hardest move of the route. The hand is cold and white, or warm and covered with hairs, and sometimes it is only the hand of a dead man seen inaccessible and rotting at the back of a crack on some eerie traverse of the Eiger, omen of a deteriorating situation — bad weather, doomed bivouacs, a glove lost, a dropped stove, a broken axe. In a pub near Oldham one night Bob Almanac told me a version in which there was no hand at all: but the crack itself closed on you and you hung there in the void unable to move up or down while the entire weight of your body slowly shifted itself on to your one trapped arm and you saw that worse than falling is not being allowed to fall. They tell it as a dream, a joke, an anecdote of the old Creagh Dhu Club, something once read. It is the expression of a deep-seated anxiety.

"What do you think of *Take it to the Edge*?" Normal asked me. "As a title?"

He stirred the sugar bowl and smiled over suddenly at the marmosets, one of whom had just said to the other, "I mean eggs."

I dreamed about climbing the wall of a warehouse in Camden Town, high above an abandoned inlet on the Grand Union Canal. Below me, rotting wooden houseboats shifted on their dirty mooring ropes, and one or two brownish ducks huddled in the cold wind on the towpath, among the dock leaves and the hedge mustard stark as a tangle of barbed wire. At the base of the wall grew ivies with strange-shaped leaves. It was coming on to rain from the south, where I could see the white confectionery fretwork of the gasometer cradles, the spire of the St Pancras Hotel. An airliner slipped across the dusty sky. Over the inlet, on the bare packed earth of the scrapyards, they were breaking up a car.

All at once I clutched the empty metal frame of a window. My heart was in my mouth. I was aware that the life was leaking tragically out of all these things.

In the middle distance where the light made it hard to tell the water from the banks I saw a man walking under a bridge, harvesting a kind of rubbery weed. I would not go back down to look. Next he offered me a handful of pink shells. Eighty feet below me his face was an indistinct oval beneath the brim of his hat. He was determined I should go down. He held up his hands and they were full of flowers — orpine, "midsummer men". A voice said, "Into the mirror to die, root and flower." Inside the empty shell of the building something tapped aimlessly and the draughts blew the dust along the floor. The window ledge creaked as I moved; it shifted a little.

I told Normal this dream, and he was silent for a minute or two. Then he nodded matter-of-factly, and with the air of someone opening up a new subject said,

"I once knew two lads who called their rope Phillip."

*

29

I had worked in London for three years. On weekdays I ate in the restaurants near the university, queuing at cinemas in the evening to see the latest French and Russian films. At the weekend I would walk along the bank of the canal to King's Cross to buy a paperback from the station bookstall; or, in the other direction, to Regent's Park or the maze of streets behind Tesco where in a heat like a kind of jelly poured in between the buildings, Greek and Turkish Cypriot widows, the shortest women I had ever seen, toiled along with bulging patchwork shopping bags and huge, slow-moving buttocks, or sat by an open door stroking a black cat.

There were cats everywhere, especially when it rained. They crouched under the shuttered railway arches among the sodden fish and chip papers off which they had already licked all the fat. They stood indecisively on the wet pavement outside the Plaza at night. They slept runny eyed but patient in shop doorways and among the piles of plastic milk crates. Everyone in London had one, dancing embarrassedly on its hind legs in the front room to snatch at a bit of tuna fish; sitting on a television staring into space. One Saturday morning I saw half a dozen old people leaning over the railings of a basement area in Pratt Street, where a cat had somehow got itself shut in the coal cellar. They had heard it clearly, they explained, but none of them could see it or get down to it: there were no steps, and no one would let them into the house.

"There it is. There it is again!"

"Oh yes, there it is again, poor thing."

"— the poor thing!"

They tilted their heads, to encourage me to listen.

"It might be hurt, you see, or anything."

"— hurt or anything!"

A diagonal shadow had been inching its way over the worn flagstones all morning and now divided the area in half. The cellar door, with its broken frosted-glass panels, was in the dark half.

Once you got over the railings, I thought, the drop would be no more than ten feet: if you stepped over, bent down facing the street, and then lowered yourself to the full length of your arms, you would be all right. I touched the railings. They were warm and rusty. I could imagine myself swinging over them, and this made me feel vaguely excited, as if I had already done it.

"I'll just go down and see," I said.

Down in the area it was cool. A mysterious vitality had caused its walls of greyish London brick to grow damp moss, and in one place small clumps of willow herb and bright yellow ragwort. If I looked back up I could see the agitated expectant heads of the old people, sweating gently in the Camden sun. I began to wonder what I would do with the cat if I caught it, and how I would get out of the area myself. Indistinct noises came from the cellar.

"Come on then puss!" I called. "Puss?"

All at once it shot out into the daylight blinking and hissing, and streaked up the wall sending down little fragments of rotten mortar.

On the pavement among the feet of the old people, trapped again, it turned and turned on itself, making a sort of bubbling angry whine and rocking back and forth on its haunches, while they backed away from it with nervous skips and jumps.

As soon as it saw a gap it ran off up Pratt Street and round a corner. It was tabby and white, quite large.

"Oh well!" I said. "Not much wrong with him!"

This fetched a laugh.

"Now," I said.

Chipped or missing bricks encouraged me to scramble up a foot or two then hang from my left while I reached out with the other for the base of the railings. I couldn't quite touch them, and I found that in this position I was pivoting away from the wall. A man kept sticking his arm through for me to catch.

"Here! Here! Let me —" he said.

He took off his coat excitedly and knelt on the pavement.

"No," I said.

I got down and started from the bottom again, extending my whole body this time instead of only my arm, so that I felt as if one long straight line could be drawn, up from the ball of my left foot to the fingertips of my right hand. I pushed down with my left hand and, as I began to swing away from the wall, got hold of the railings easily and tugged hard. "Here!" shouted the man who had stuck his arm through. He fussed over me as I stepped back over on to the pavement, patting my sleeves and dusting my shoulders.

"*There* you come!" he said, looking around as if he'd pulled me up after all.

I was wheeling a trolley round one of the supermarkets in Camden High Street when an old lady came up to me very determinedly and stood in my way. "I think it was a wonderful thing you did," she said. "And I hope they put you in the papers for it."

She rubbed her eyes.

Two or three weeks later someone I knew rang me up and asked me if I would like to go and learn rock-climbing in the sports centre at Holloway. Remembering how easy and pleasant it had been to reach up, lock off my arm, then pull hard at the base of the railings so that I was suddenly lifted almost without effort back into the street, I said yes. I was about thirty years old.

At Hoghton Quarry the rhododendron flowers are a strange transparent lilac colour. They drift down past you as you climb, like confetti at the marriage of air and rock, while below you the tall straight trees filter out the light from the boggy aisle in front of the cliff. There are rhododendron bushes on every ledge, and when you are trying to get off the top you have to make your way down through a plantation of them, slithering helplessly about with the steep friable brown soil caking your feet and your nose full of their oppressive dusty smell, you clutch at the tangled stems with mounting hysteria.

"Those," said Normal when I mentioned them, "are the rhododendrons of an Earl. They are an *Earl's* rhododendrons, and those are his trees."

Normal had taken two or three of us up there in his car to try and free the remaining aid moves on a climb called Boadicea. We were trespassing. Hoghton is a secluded, impressive place whose pale sandy walls stretch above you, some as concave as the bow of a battleship, others raddled with enormous silent overhangs. Birds give piping calls in the green twilight. Between the fallen quarry buildings and overgrown hummocks the ground is spongy with sphagnum. There is a fur of lichen on everything; it gives an air of intimacy, but you don't welcome intimacy on such a scale. You eye the huge corroded bolts sticking out of the rock: your gaze is drawn up further than it wants to go. Every silent figure you see among the trees might be the Earl, breathing heavily but quietly — watching. We had no luck with Boadicea, and towards evening rain began to rustle down between the leaves and drip into our little colourful heaps of equipment.

To get to the quarry you go over a railway line, then walk up a marshy slot. On the way back through the wet fields, Normal pointed gravely at everything as he named it: grass, fences, walls, all belonged to the Earl of Hoghton. A grey mist came up out of the distant woods. When we got to the place where you cross the railway he made us stop while he studied the signals intently, then he flopped down and put his ear to one of the rails.

"Nothing coming," he said.

In the village where we had parked the car he told us, "This is the *village* of an Earl. How do you like it? These are an Earl's flowers, this is his chapel — Wesleyan — and this is *the telephone box of an Earl*." He spread his arms wide. Rain drummed on the roof of the car. We were soaked. "Above is the fucking leaky sky of an Earl!"

On the way home he pointed out barns and hedgerows that he said belonged to the Earl.

"Are those the cows of the Earl?" I asked.

"No."

"But that's his chemical factory?"

"No it isn't."

There was scaffolding under all the motorway bridges in the north that year. The signs were being changed. That night, lost among the contraflow systems around Bolton, we watched the heavy vehicles nose past with water smoking away from under their mudguards and their loads wrapped in blue and orange tarpaulin.

"Is this the A666?"

"It says 'Back Lorne Street'."

Finally, as we went through Salford, Normal swerved the car in towards the pavement and pointed his finger at a dark furry mess in the gutter.

"*That*," he said, "was the cat of an Earl."

This was the year after I had left London, and I had a cat of my own.

I had just met Normal, who was still working at High Adventure, in Manchester, lounging yellow in the face with boredom every day behind a glass counter, while the rain blowing down Deansgate made white streaks on the windows and his customers argued desultorily over the merits of a hank of fluorescent rope from Italy, or leafed through the autobiography of a famous mountaineer they thought they had once seen. "Adventure," promised the neon sign above the main window, "High Adventure".

By then I lived in one of the solid red ironmaster houses that are set foursquare behind laurel hedges all along the main roads into Stalybridge and Ashton. The earth in the back garden was stamped bare and strewn with charred mattresses, but had once a huge tree which drooped over my balcony. At night I would go out there with the cat. A smell of laburnum came remote and tranquil from some other garden. The balcony was full of dry stalks and leaves flaking down to powder. The cat sprang and pounced among them, or sat still suddenly and purred. There was a shout from the main road, then a note or two of music. I would stroke the cat absentmindedly.

The old man in the flat downstairs from me kept his door open so that the sharp smell of cooked vegetables soaked into the warm air of his landing. The bathroom, which was shared, was on his floor, and as soon as you got into the bath he was knocking to say that he had to use the lavatory. He waited on the stairs if he heard your door open or close, and let milk boil over late at night. The first day I was there he came up and told me he was on his own, his daughter had gone out without leaving him anything to eat.

"She usually leaves me something," he said. "A bit of ham or something. Are you having some tea?"

"No," I said, "but I could make you a cup of coffee," and he stood in my kitchen looking at the orange plastic breadbin I had bought that day, while I boiled the kettle and got two cups out. "It'll only be instant," I said.

Did he take sugar? He liked a bit of sugar. Milk? Not too much.

34

He had a kind of weak pliability but once he began to stare at something he seemed to go into a dream.

"I don't want to intrude," he said.

"I'm always busy in the evenings," I said. "Here you are."

"If you haven't got any tea," he said.

He forced his eyes away from the breadbin.

"I can't have coffee. We never have coffee."

I said that I had some Chinese tea somewhere, but he wouldn't have that either. After a minute or two standing there he left the room slowly. I poured the Nescafe down the sink and swilled the cup out, feeling angry but relieved. Then I heard him coming back again.

"I'll have to wait for my daughter then. She went without me seeing. Could you give me a slice of bread to be going on with?"

I banged the breadbin open, cut him two slices of bread and put butter on them. Without looking at him I said, "They're wholemeal. You probably prefer white. Oh, and you'll want a plate."

"Thank you," he said. "They're thicker than I like."

I heard him talking to himself as he went down. After that I kept my door locked even when I was in, and if I heard him on the stairs stopped whatever I was doing until he'd gone. He never knocked, but he would sometimes shuffle round for hours on the landing outside, pretending to sweep the lino.

If I had milk delivered, he took it. When I went to get it back I saw that the furniture in his rooms, inert great armchairs and sideboards with cracked and lifting veneers, was hidden under a drift of letters he had also stolen over the years — circulars, bills, cards, small parcels, anything that had come through the door for a tenant who had died or moved away. He gave pride of place to some postcards addressed to him from Australia, and this was how I discovered that his daughter had married and emigrated there sixteen years ago. "She was ungrateful," he said. "She was an ungrateful girl." He avoided my eyes and stared at the television, an old black and white set with a screen like a fishbowl. He kept it on all day: and in the summer when he couldn't sleep the sirens of phantasmal foreign police cars hee-hawed through the night until I banged and banged on his door.

He hated the cat.

"Bloody filthy dirty thing," he said. "I was trying to get rid of it before you came."

I caught him making feeble pushing motions at it on the stairs.

It *was* a dirty cat. It never seemed to lose its dense, oily kitten fur, which soon became spiky and matted. It was smallish, very black, and it pulled its food about all over the kitchen floor, running up suddenly to snatch a piece out of the saucer, coughing and snorting loudly as it ate. When it had finished it would come and sit on the arm of the chair and butt its forehead into yours, purring and breathing the smell of fish and liver into your face. I watched it trying to catch flies in the dim washy light after a thunderstorm. One of them escaped it and walked about in repetitive loops on the wall, its shadow preceding it. The cat clicked and mewed with rage.

"You leave it alone," I warned the old man. "And don't take milk that isn't yours."

I still loved for their own sake the look and feel of the things you use for climbing: the clear, sharp-edged, almost fluorescent colour of a length of brand-new nylon tape as Normal pulled it off the reel at four o'clock on a dark winter afternoon, the bitter smell it made when he burned the end to seal it, the thick complex knot you had to tie in it to employ it as a sling. I loved the weight and polish of a figure-of-eight descender when you picked it up in the shop, a great mass of forged aluminium alloy designed to channel the heat away from the rope as you shot down it a hundred feet clear like a spider on the end of its string; or, whooping and shouting, pushed yourself out from the cliff in gigantic leaps and bounds as you dropped. I loved the light they seemed to generate, orange, blue, neapolitan lime, a glitter like chrome; and the memory they brought back, like a physical event, of the climbs I had done a week or a month before.

I went to High Adventure whenever I could. I tried on and bought this harness or that pair of boots. Normal watched with a kind of amused benevolence from behind the counter. I encouraged him to talk. Often he would turn up where I lived on a Friday night to lend me a book or show me a photograph of a new climb. One night he told me about a climber he knew called Ed, who had made a reputation in the Lake District while he earned his living as a beach photographer at Morecambe.

Ed had found it a good business, Normal said. All you needed for it was a reasonable camera and a monkey: there was a small grey type with clean fur that would sit fairly quietly on your shoulder even in a crowd, and in general the beach photographers used that. The idea was to get among the people on the sea front so that the women and children spotted the monkey. As soon as one of them picked it up or made a fuss of it — snap!

"'Like the photo, madam?'" Normal mimicked. "'I'll post it on. One of the kiddy? Ten quid to you!'"

"Ten pounds?" I said. I didn't know how much of this was Normal's fantasy. "How did he get away with it?"

Normal looked into his coffee.

"Oh you rarely got one that wouldn't pay," he said vaguely but with a suggestion of menace. Then something made him laugh. "People like a monkey until they find out about its habits."

"I suppose so."

Ed was at Morecambe for two or three seasons running. He found that he could make enough in a day to live, and enough in two or three to live well. When he was out on the front he wore to attract attention to himself a velvet coat a nice colour of maroon, cut very long and flared, and a green neckscarf. He had his Olympus OM–1 round his neck and the monkey, attached to a length of shiny chain, on his shoulder. The monkey, Normal said, had a strange smell when you got close to it, strong but not unpleasant, and its fur had in some lights a real green tinge. Ed looked very smart, on the whole; very smart indeed. The older women loved him.

"But guess what he had on his feet?"

"I don't know," I said.

"Rock boots," said Normal. "He had his rock boots on! Because when he'd made his money for the day, he'd go down on to the sand and do slab problems on the sea wall!" He chuckled reminiscently. "Have you seen the size of that sea wall? He was a mad bugger, Ed."

Everyone Normal knew was mad. It was a diploma he awarded without reserve. When I met Ed later I found that he was a fattish powerful man, rather quiet and withdrawn, who still climbed very well indeed though he was less interested in it than he had been. Every time I saw him in the Peak District, picking his way up Artless or Downhill Racer or one of the other unprotected gritstone climbs there, I thought of the little grey complaisant monkey, and the children on Morecambe pier watching mystifiedly as Ed worked out careful balancey moves five feet up on the flaking concrete of the steep but minute sea wall: shifting his weight slowly, slowly, then scuttling crabwise up to grasp the thick polished railings at the top and heave himself over with a satisfied grin. "Like the photo, madam?"

"Does he still do it?" I asked Normal.

"No."

"What happened to the monkey?"

"I don't know," he said. "I think it hung itself in its chain one day." And he got up to rinse his cup out in the sink. When he had finished he said, "How's the cat?"

I couldn't tell. It was ill. It was eating as greedily as ever then vomiting the food up in fits which frightened and disgusted me. It crouched on the living room floor, coughing out fur balls and swallowing them again in great bronchitic heaves, staring warily at me in case I put it outside the door. During the close, thundery afternoons it sidled about under the furniture and was sick by the bookshelves. I was always too late: a rhythmic gulping sound, a croak, a grey puddle spreading on the carpet. Between these fits it purred and watched the flies, much as it had always done. I discovered that the old man had begun to feed it fishbones from the side of his plate.

I cornered him on the landing outside his flat. It had been a long hot day and a foul smell hung in the air. Over his thin sloping shoulder I could see into his front room. Thick piles of hair-clippings lay on the pocked green lino. He cut his hair himself, and often left it there for days on end. Through his window was a view of the road, where a few children were playing desultorily on bicycles. On the wall opposite, one of them had chalked, "Whoever redes this is a cunt."

"You must never give it fishbones," I explained patiently. "It will choke on them."

"I can't stop it stealing, can I?" he complained. "Cats eat fish. The poor little thing."

He licked his lips and watched me. He had on a cotton vest, wrinkled over a pot belly peculiarly swollen and hard. His arms were thin — though they had once been muscular — the skin loose and sore in the creases of his elbow. I noticed that his hands were trembling slightly. Suddenly I had had enough of him.

"You know bloody well it isn't the cat that's stealing!" I shouted in his face. I was trembling too. "It's ill. It's ill, you stupid old idiot!"

I stepped round him and went quickly through his door. I was practised at this. Every day I had to get my milk back, or look for my letters. I had caught him with my groceries. I had caught him with a dish of Kit-E-Kat Meat & Liver Dinner. "It's filthy in here," I said. "Can't you clean it up a bit? I can smell it from upstairs when you open the door." He came in behind me and stood in the twilight biting his lips, his weak eyes sliding sideways to the television screen, which showed a factory, a mechanical process of one sort or another, and then a man driving down a road on a housing estate.

"And another thing," I said. "You can keep *that* thing turned down."

I prodded him in the stomach.

He looked at me and swallowed. "If you do that I'll shit myself," he said.

"Christ."

I only ever went to Morecambe once.

Even though it was late in the day the sky was like brass. I had been climbing all through July further up the coast. I remember the placid muddy water of the boating pool, beyond which rotting piles go out into some great slow tidal stream slipping past to join the Kent Channel; sleeping women on the sand, their dresses pulled up to expose their thighs to the thick hot light; the giant cone above the ice cream stall. In a fish restaurant they advertised "best butter" on the bread. A man finished his meal then stared ahead with his mouth open while two teenage couples took snaps of each other across the table with a cheap camera. Music hung in the air in the amusement park, with diesel smoke and the smell of fried onions. "Blue Moon, now I'm no longer alone." A dog trotted by. Nobody was playing Catch-a-Duck.

I felt relaxed and elated both at once. The heat, the smells, the music, the signs on the sea front might all have been one thing, one stimulus appealing to a simple sensory organ we all used to have but have now forgotten we possess.

All the time Ed was there he dreamed of South America.

At a BMC lecture in Lancaster two or three years earlier he had overheard the visiting speaker say, "Magnetic anomalies affected our compass . . ." and then later the same evening ". . . at sunset, behind the Col Mirador." Attracted by these two strange half-sentences, which afterwards became joined in his mind, he started to read widely in mountaineering accounts of Cerro Torre, Roraima, the Towers of Paine; and to collect expensive early editions of Whymper and Shipton. "We put a camp in the lee of the small moraine there, and began to fix ropes." But he soon found it wasn't the climbing that interested him so much as the unearthliness of the place itself.

In 1895 evidence had turned up at Last Hope Inlet near Puerto Natales, Chile, of a ground-living sloth the size of a rhinoceros. Found in conjunction with human remains, it had died only recently. It had perhaps been domesticated. Only just discovered, it was only just extinct . . . in fact the Tehuelche Indians believed it could still be found alive. It was nocturnal, they said, covered with coarse hair; and it had huge hooked claws.

Because of this blurring-together of geological and historical time, plants as well as animals teetered on the brink. "The puya," Ed read, "is a living fossil. With its inturned spines it can imprison and kill a small dog as easily as a bird. The Indians burn it wherever they find it, so that their young children are not at risk." The Andean landscapes, too, had a curious central equivocality: black ignimbrite plains above Ollague like spill from some vast recently abandoned mine: the refurbished pre-Inca irrigation canals near Machu Picchu, indistinguishable from mountain streams. Half-seen outlines, half-glimpsed possibilities; and to set against them, a desperate clarity of the air. Cerro Puntiagudo hung, with its snowfields like a feather necklace, in a sky blue enough to make your teeth ache.

Ed never went there.

He would have liked to do a climb in the Paine National Park. He thought of following the itinerary of the Hesketh-Prichard expedition, which at the turn of the century had gone in search of a living megatherium only to falter before it even reached Last Hope and turn for home furious and dispirited. He had always meant to go. Somehow he was never able to save the money; or, if he did, his friends let him down. The Falklands Crisis intervened. He turned to the television natural history programmes, where a chance alignment of rock peaks nearly broke his heart.

The pictures were so clear. He caught his breath as the camera swooped up and burst over this ridge or that to reveal San Pedro, Licancabur or the Los Patos Pass beyond, then raced over flat and stony plains covered with strange tussocks of grass and fading into the purplish line of the volcanoes; or dwelt on the death of a guanaco foal beneath the Paine Towers. He blinked back tears at the sound of pan-pipes, because something in it brought the entire Andes to him like a scent on the wind. It was a kind of nostalgia, but for a place you have never been. Through the open window at night he heard not the funfair, though he could easily see its wheeling lights, but the wind lifting the soil off the stony terraces of the Inca Altiplano. He would tease the monkey gently with his forefinger, whispering to it, "We placed bolts in the Red Dierdre, the sandstone girdle, the exit ramps . . . The wooden box with the wireless set and microscope slides is missing . . . Today as we retreated from the ice bulge I felt so far away from home . . ." Generally it was calmed by this, but sometimes instead it would be goaded into an infantile fury and race round the room screeching and chattering and tearing up his photographs.

Taking a film out of his OM–1 at mid-day in August, he would be ambushed by memories of the Atacama he had never seen.

Punta Arenas lay in wait for him at the end of Morecambe Pier.

Always just out of sight, the sixty-metre ice cliffs of the San Rafael Glacier glittered in the sun, calving into a green and milky sea.

Slowly he realised it was not the real South America he loved but some continent of his own invention.

After Normal left High Adventure and moved to Huddersfield, where his wife had the offer of a local authority job that would support them both, there was nothing to keep me in Stalybridge. The work I was doing meant nothing to me. Normal got a house on an estate. Since he was the only person in the north I knew well, I thought I might as well go and rent a cheap cottage in one of the valleys that run down from the moors south and west of the town. I didn't want to live on a housing estate.

By that time my cat had died, though not from eating the old man's fish bones. It ran in from the street one morning with the left side of its lower jaw broken, and lay sprawled and panting on the mat. The eye on that side had been pushed in, causing it to turn and lift its head irritably every so often, as if it could see something through it that wasn't there. A car had run it over I suppose. Sick cats often hide in the garden or crouch all day just out of reach under a cupboard: but they always know when a human being is their only chance. I kept it alive for two or three days, even though the vet recommended putting it down. In the end I had to give up. While I was trying to get it to drink something it looked up at me, with the broken jaw making a kind of fragile snarl, and purred. I didn't know whether this was from pain — out of some desperate failure of vocabulary — or affection. Either way I remembered it butting its forehead against mine after it had eaten its dinner, and I couldn't bear that.

When I left Stalybridge the old man was still going strong. Oddly enough he never seemed to understand that the cat was dead. For a long time afterwards I would hear him on the stairs in the evenings, calling "Puss! Puss!", or in the mornings find a saucer of thin grey milk outside his door.

4 · SANKEY'S VIEW

After each thaw the view from the upstairs window became much bleaker. The snow retreated to the edge of the fields and lay there piled up against the low stone walls. Everything had a curiously unfinished look. Sheep picked their way over the steep fields in single file, unnerved by the re-emergence of this forgotten landscape. The old poached places reappeared at gates, black against the bruised grass. Nothing could yet be said to be green. It was less quiet. Starlings sat up in the house gutters and on the telephone wires to do poor, cracked imitations of other birds; after each effort, sneers, whistles and a kind of rhythmical creaking or scraping noise broke out. Later every afternoon as the days grew longer, the sodium lights came on on the other side of the valley, grouped in twos and threes near farms, following the line of a road. In the fading light the wooded cloughs struck diagonally across the hillside, very black and immobile. The next time he looked up it had all gone quite black, and only the orange lights were left.

5 · MARCH, IN THE END

In the end March was useless.

We weren't getting the weather, Bob Almanac said. Without that the year was in abeyance, its whole business untransactable. We raced into the dazzling sun of the cold mornings, looking for signs that the door was swinging open for us. But a grey light lay on the beech trees, and the walls and farmhouses had the bleached

43

look sunlight gives them deep in the winter. One day I saw a warm tobacco-brown haze on the moors to the south of Buxton.

"It looks nice."

"Wait till you get out of the car. It'll freeze your bollocks off. What's the capital of Louisiana?"

"I don't know."

"I thought you were educated."

The sun had always gone in by the time we got where we were going. The rock was bitter. Down in Staffordshire knuckles of it break out of the tops of the ridges in the mist, like the rocks in a Hammer film. The wind sweeps up from the Potteries over isolated farms where they are committing incest or parricide or staring into an empty cup listening to the abandoned machinery and banging gates outside.

"What's it like up there?"

"Piss wet through."

"I mean, what's the climbing like?"

"All right if you're a duck."

Bits of hail bounced along the slanting ledges like bone dice. After half an hour it settled in. It melted on the holds and from each one a little dribble of cold water started down the dry lichenous rock like a tear. Another Saturday fucked.

Smashed black blocks of rock balanced on one another like the remains of some civilisation whose observances grew so monolithic that in the end there was nothing to do but fall back into error, decline, barbarism. Easy enough to say what sends you away from here feeling so defeated. The weather, the moor, the greenish lichen on everything. Everything turns to paste when you touch it, says Bob Almanac, disgustedly scratching his head. Even the bones are green here, dead sheep scattered empty-socketed at the bottom of a stony gully. The climbs seem wilful. You ebb away into the valley.

"Clocks change soon then."

"Why?"

"What do you mean: why? You great wazzock, the *clocks* change soon. It'll be British Summer Time in a week!"

"Oh. I thought you said, 'Pog's changed his tune.'"

"Who's Pog?"

I ran over Black Hill every morning to keep fit. For three days the valleys were full of freezing fog. From above you could see it lying pure white and motionless in the sun. Going down into it you found it grey, without comfort. A tree stood on the interface, bare and thorny. Inside, frost covered everything: before you had run a mile it had formed in your hair and beard, on the fibres of your clothes. Distances were shortened, sounds muffled. You went on in silence and the sheep lifted their heads to stare.

I was still at the indoor wall once or twice a week. I always went on Tuesday or Wednesday, in the afternoon when I would be unlikely to find other climbers there. The problems seemed as hard as they had done in January, but I thought I was getting stronger. I wasn't panicking so much, either, when things went wrong. After half an hour or so I would sit on the floor flexing my fingers and listening to the weight lifters who worked in an area near the wall. (Climbers had been forbidden this area because they had sneaked into it so often without paying.) They groaned like invalids. They addressed their apparatus, with all its springs and counterweights, like lovers. They moved off deeper into it, browsing placidly, so that you saw them like elephants or oxen through a screen of trees.

Sometimes they smiled at me patiently, wondering perhaps why anybody so thin would come here at all.

Waiting for some signal I sat tiredly on the gymnasium floor, watching the traffic through the long windows, the light on the polished but dusty floor. I waited for the bus back to Huddersfield. A few crushed looking Pakistanis got off it and went away into the cold. From the top deck of the bus I could look down at the monumental stone houses set slightly back off the road, with their flat bare lawns and neat tarmac paths like those in the grounds of a mental home or a crematorium. Factories, cottages, terraces, then a vista of fields opening out to a viaduct; a sudden smell of acetone on the bus.

That Saturday I said, "I think it's Memphis."

"What?"

"The capital of Louisiana."

We were racing the weather down to Miller's Dale. March is the hinge. There is always the sense that the year might as easily slam shut on it as open.

45

PART TWO

SPRING

6 · MASTERS OF THE MODERN DANCE

In April I fell off a route at Stanage Edge.

A new kind of rock boot had come on to the market. Manufactured from the rubber compound used in Formula One tyres, the soles of these boots were supposed to give considerably improved friction on slabs and in all the situations where footwork was important. Their disadvantage was that they were hard to come by; and they were so badly designed they were painful to wear. Some climbers were sceptical about the claims made for them; others believed, it was not clear why, that they should be reserved for experts, ordinary boots being good enough for anyone else. I had some and I wanted to try them out. The suede uppers were a beautiful shade of bluish grey, the laces wine red. I had had a pair of size seven shoe trees in them for a week to stretch them.

Normal went first.

The route began with some painful finger-jamming round an undercut, then he had to turn a series of big featureless overhangs which forced him diagonally to the right across the front of the buttress. It was very strenuous. He got some protection in a horizontal break, hissing and puffing with nerves as he hung from his right hand and sorted with his left through the wires and tapes clipped to his harness until he found something that would fit. After that his strength began to fade and his progress was fragmentary, full of stoppages and wrong decisions. "You're on your arms all the time!" he complained, tucking his feet up under him and scraping at the rock with first one and then the other to try and spread his weight. By the time he had wrestled his way back left and worked out how to use the short finishing crack, his forearms were pumped up like Popeye the Sailor's, and I had to lower him off on the rope.

He stood at the bottom, panting and looking up.

"You're on your arms all the time," he repeated.

He shook his head.

"All the time. It wouldn't be so bad if it wasn't for that."

He tried twice more but couldn't do it and came down each time massaging his hands, depressed at the waste of all this energy.

"I'll get the runners out later," he said. "I'll abseil down for them after I've had a rest."

I was lighter than Normal. I thought I could accept the logic of the rightward movement round the overhangs and not fight against it.

"Leave them in," I said. "I want to try."

He stared at me surprisedly. Then he laughed.

"You and those bloody boots!"

I shrugged.

He knew I had never led anything so hard before, and he seemed to be discussing it with himself. "I suppose it can't hurt," he said, then: "All right, why not? Give it a go." He undid from the rope — we were using a doubled nine millimetre — and handed me the end. "Get tied on to that before I change my mind." He rummaged through his sack until he found the Thermos flask. He always had his tea without milk. "You'll be quite good if you can do anything with the crack," he promised me, gazing out over the valley.

I went round picking up my bits and pieces; I hung them on my harness.

"You won't need those," Normal said. "The gear's good. You could drop a Ford Fiesta on that top runner. You could drop an elephant on it."

After all, I thought: I've got the boots.

By then I was planning one or two moves, a show of courage, a graceful retreat. But the undercut gave way as soon as I pulled up and I was so surprised I began to scuttle right as quickly as I could, after the deteriorating handholds. Suddenly it was no effort. I could smell the damp bracken; and the curious spicy odour of the gritstone in front of my face. I could feel the new boots, edging on a tiny quartz pebble, clinging magisterially to nothing; and my hands as they selected and rejected a finger-pocket, a little rib, a large rounded hole like a bucket which worked in the wrong direction to be any use. It was exhilarating. I was the idea or intuition that sat cleverly at the centre of all this, directing it.

I remembered clearly being in the swimming baths as a boy. The tiled edge was slimy, the steps steep, the water glutinous and lifeless about me. Everyone else could swim. I was cold. I patrolled slowly from one side of the shallow end to the other. I made swimming motions, but only to feel the water slapping under my chin. I was half-hearted, I expected nothing. But then intention and action became somehow confused and I was shooting forward over the surface in a way I did not understand. It was some time before I related this sensation to the idea of swimming; after that I never felt it with quite the same purity and sharpness . . .

At the base of the finishing crack, dependent on an astonishingly painful hand-jam while I fought to get one foot on a sloping ledge somewhere at the level of my chest, I heard Normal shout,

"Don't give up! It's yours now! It's yours!"

He was delighted. When I looked down I could see his face, gleaming and mad. He groaned. He called, "Go on, go on! I've never seen you climb like this!"

The last runner he had put in was four feet below me. The same distance above me was the top, a few clumps of grass and bilberry hanging over a dusty, rounded edge. "Go on then," shouted Normal, "just reach through. Just reach through!" The hand-jam plopped out without any warning, and then I was dangling a bit dazed on the end of the rope, blood coming out of my nose where I had banged it on the rock. My hand looked as if it had been through a food processor.

"Bastard!" said Normal. He had hit his head on the undercut when the impact of the fall jerked him off his feet. "Why did you do that? It was yours!"

I still felt elated.

"I nearly had it," I said. "I nearly had it!"

As I hung there gently turning from side to side I could see right along the edge in both directions. It was about half past eleven on a

Saturday morning. Great strings of ramblers were already trailing up and down the worn stones of the Roman path, coloured like the paper tails of kites. "Cut that noise down," the school parties had been warned as they left the minibus, "and remember you're out for a day in the country." The new boots had begun to pinch my toes.

"Are these things supposed to wear a hole in your foot?" I called down to Normal.

He climbed it in the end.

He solved the crux by attacking the overhangs direct, in a sustained savage burst of effort which eliminated most of the protection. In that form it was beyond anything I could do.

"It's a trip, that," was his judgement.

His hands trembled with adrenalin-shock: he studied them puzzledly. Under the impression it hadn't been climbed before, I wanted him to name it The Magic Boots; Normal, though, favoured Peanut Power. We soon learned that a team from Sheffield had snapped it up at the end of the previous November.

"What did they call it?"

"Masters of the Modern Dance. The fucking wimps."

The local climbers describe any fall that ends on the ground as "decking it". Elsewhere a fall like that might be known as a "crater"; it depends where you are.

Normal boasted about his own falls, particularly the one he took from the railway train, which put him in plaster for a whole summer: but he had a prim attitude to other people's.

One day near the end of April Sankey, who used to tie on to the end of the rope with a peculiar home-made waistbelt which transferred the shock load of the fall directly on to his kidneys and diaphragm, misjudged a move high up over the pool at Lawrencefield Quarry. Fifteen feet above and to the side of his runner, he swung across the wall like the pendulum of a clock and with a mournful clatter of equipment and an explosion of chalk smashed into a shoulder of rock at right angles to it.

After a short silence he said, "Let me down quick."

Normal laughed grimly when he heard about this.

"Sankey's losing his touch," he said. "What route was it?" I told him and he said:

"Two years ago he'd have pissed up that. Pissed up it."

Not long after I got the magic boots we were back at Stanage. A climber from Rotherham was stretchered off before we had been there half an hour.

He had lost his momentum thirty feet up a blunt fin of rock when he found himself bridged out between the arête and a smallish foothold on the face. The effort of sustaining the bridge made his legs shake. He called something down to his second and shifted his feet as far as his situation would allow. This eased the strain on his thigh muscles and gave him enough confidence to pat, pat, pat with his free hand, looking for any tiny hold which might lever him out of the bridge and help him shift his weight on to the face. Soon his legs started to shake again. He looked down desperately as if to impress on himself the distance to the ground and called to his friend, "I'll have to put my feet back, it's no good, they were better where they were —" By the time we noticed him it was clear he had been through this cycle three or four times. He had tried and failed to place a runner. He was beginning to tire. He would not find the hold he wanted. To Normal he was just a figure in faded red tracksuit trousers, a T-shirt bearing the legend Pacific Ironworks: near enough to see but too far off for sympathy.

"It looks quite hard," I said.

"He won't do it now," Normal predicted. "He's already blown it. You don't bridge that, you just step across." He got into his harness, inspected the buckle disgustedly. "I'm chucking this away when I get home," he promised. "It's been buggered for a year."

"I don't think I can work this out," said the boy from Rotherham.

By now everyone but Normal was staring up and giving conflicting advice. If one said, "Sort that runner out and get a move on!" there was another to tell him to forget it. "If you go back to the arête you can have a rest." Aware that his private misery had become public, and tiring as much as anything else of the social and intellectual pressure to find a solution, he gave up and tried to take all his weight on his right hand. We watched him swing gently outwards, like a door opening, and slip off. He fell among the boulders with what in other circumstances might have been a sigh of relief. Afterwards, strapped to the Thomas stretcher, he reminded me of a chrysalis, primed and pupating.

His friend went bounding down the hill in front of him carrying both their rucksacks, full of that queer nervous energy which often embarrasses you in those situations, quartering the slopes like a spaniel in the winter bracken, looking back over his shoulder at the stretcher bearers as if for encouragement; while a small ambulance drove up and down the road below, sometimes flashing its blue light at the moorland sheep. He was a tall, fair boy, about eighteen years old, who looked as if he had the makings of a good athlete.

Later the foil blanket which had covered the casualty caught the light as someone folded it up. By that time the ambulance was going back to Sheffield, not at a great rate, and we had started climbing again.

"I didn't see blood," I said. "Do you think it was bad?"

"Keep your eye on the rope," Normal recommended quietly. "I'm on the hard bit."

He was a long way above me but the wet air gave his voice close, conversational qualities. He stood up delicately on one toe and with his back curved in a strange, graceful S-shape reached for the rounded holds at the top. "They're here," he explained. "But they're awkward to use." When it was my turn the rock looked very black.

We climbed all day. Rags of mist came up through the plantation, where a kind of humid softness or distinctness of the air made the trees seem as if they were hiding something, and the rock never really dried out; but though it threatened to rain it never did. All day long the cement factory above Hope pumped heavy moist smoke straight up into the cloudbase, then at nightfall it vanished without warning, to be replaced on the obscure hillside by a constellation of orange lamps which suggested the shape of an ocean liner.

"Never mind that," said Normal. "Let's get to the pub."

Though it looks remote, and in some lights romantic, Stanage is only two miles from the suburbs of Sheffield. When the wind is right you can smell dinners cooking in the Kelvin Flats.

54

7 · GAZ & SANKEY

An awkward grinning lad called Gaz worked at the butcher's in the town. You often saw him at dinner time, a head taller than anyone else in the street, clumping over the zebra crossing by the health food shop in the steel-trimmed work clogs favoured by generations of local slaughtermen, his red hair cut in a kind of savage brush. He was eighteen or twenty. He had transport, a fawn Vauxhall which he sometimes drove like a maniac. When he spoke he made aggressive bobbing movements of his head and shoulders; this was out of shyness. He was always impatient to get to the crag, and he came out with one or another of us whenever he could take a day off.

At the beginning of May he and I went to Trowbarrow Quarry in Lancashire, where I wanted to try a route called The Coral Sea. Coral Sea is fun not because it is hard but because it's a steep slab covered with tiny delicate fossil imprints, so that you are climbing even more than usual on a kind of frozen time. We found that ICI had closed it and put up trespass warnings. We wandered about anyway to emphasise what we thought of as our clear right to be there, scuffing the wood sorrel and craning our necks in astonishment at the evil zinc-grey face of the old workings. "It's meant to be limestone, but it never looks like it to me," said Gaz. "All the books say it is but it never looks like it to me." Trowbarrow Main Wall, a hundred feet high, totters on one pediment of rock: as it slips inevitably away to the right, Jean Jeanie, Cracked Actor, Warspite Direct, all the cracklines are widening stealthily . . .

"You just can't settle down in a place when it's banned," he complained.

He went twenty feet up the oppressive Red Wall in his torn and dusty running shoes; warned himself, "Oops! Don't look down!"; jumped off with a thud and stared sulkily across at the abandoned explosives store with its fringe of rank weeds.

"Looks like bloody *Dr Who*."

Earth, 1997: everyone lives under the ground and wears identical clothes. Something appalling has been done to their sexuality and they walk round staring directly ahead of themselves. "Not much different to now." Every fifteen minutes a voice like the station announcer at Preston says something nobody can understand and they all walk off down a different corridor. Can the Doctor help them?

"For fuck's sake shut up," said Gaz, "and let's go somewhere we can *climb*."

Though the climbs were easier we had a much better time at Jack Scout Cove, a narrow defile at the end of a caravan site which opens out on the sudden shocking spaces of Morecambe Bay near Silverdale. As you face the sea the cliff goes up on your left, whitish, dusted with the same lichen you can see on any other limestone crag, say at Giggleswick or Malham: custard yellow, dry and crusty. You get to the top among the yew trees bent and shaved by the sea wind.

I had been there once as a boy. I knew that, but you couldn't say I remembered it.

The right bank of the cove is a clinted slab overgrown with whin, short turf and hawthorn bushes. From there the tourists can gaze out to sea or at the weed-covered rocks at the base of the cliff like green chenille cushions in the front room of a fussy old woman. They murmur and laugh, their children shout. When Gaz and I were there the hawthorn wasn't yet in blossom. Sheep moved about on the turf.

"You see those green tags in their ears?" said Gaz. "I'll be cutting them out on Monday morning. One quick slit of the knife and out they come!"

"For Christ's sake Gaz."

"I could get you some eyes to put in people's beer."

They have given the climbs in this cosy place queer existentialist names, Victim of Life, Unreal City, Lemmingsville.

"What's *your* name Louise?" asked one little girl confidingly of another.

Gaz got out his cheap denim shorts and faded Union Jack T-shirt and undressed shyly. The women eyed him. They were out from Leeds and Bradford for Whit Week by the sea, with their bare red shoulders and untalkative husbands. Gaz's arms and legs were

56

peculiarly white, as if he spent all week in the cold store. He always looked underfed but full of uncontrollable energy.

"Mummy, those men are in *our cave*!"

We traversed the whole cliff a few feet above the tideline, our shadows bobbing on the rock, dwarfing then stretching themselves, sending out an elongated arm or leg. All morning the water rose steadily, the colour of the water in the Manchester Ship Canal. "You wouldn't like to fall in that," said Gaz. And then: "What are these fucking little shrimps doing up here?" Laying away off a big white flake with his feet tucked negligently up and to one side so that he looked as intelligent as a gibbon, he probed about one-handed in a narrow crack full of things like lice with long springy tails. Suddenly he shrieked and threw himself backwards into the air, landing in the sea with a huge splash. When he came up blowing and laughing the children stared at him in exasperation. He said: "One of them jumped in me eye! Right in me eye!" He rubbed his face vigorously.

Whenever anybody mentioned Jake Scout Cove after that he would wink at me laboriously and say, "Those fucking shrimps, eh?"

In the afternoon we lay on the clints in the sun. The tourists accepted us companionably. The tide was on its way out and a transistor radio somewhere down on the damp sand played "Green Tambourine".

When you hear an old song again like that, one you have not thought about for years, there is a brief slippage of time, a shiver, as if something had cut down obliquely through your life and displaced each layer by its own depth along the fault line. Without warning I was able to recall being in Silverdale as a child. In the cafe hung a picture by a local water colourist, of two rowing boats apparently moored in a low-lying street: he wanted eleven pounds for it but it was worth more. I sat rigid with delight beneath it, a thick slab of steak and kidney pie cooling on an oval plate in front of me. "Eat your lunch, eat your lunch." Great channels of slowly moving water in the mud; strange flat peninsulas with the sheep chewing the tough grass; the empty thin hull of a crab in a pool shaped like a waving boy.

At about four o'clock Gaz sat up and clapped his hand to his face. "Fucking sunbathing!" he said. "I'm going to regret this tomorrow." And he examined gloomily the reddening patches on his thighs. "Better get going I suppose." We drove to Junction 28 on the M6, where we squatted at the base of a wall in our patched baggy tracksuit trousers and headbands, like the remains of a punitive expedition gone native among the tribes in the killing humidity. "Junction 28," runs the advert, "the best place to eat sleep and be merry." Everything was closed. Only the takeaway was open, and they had no Danish pastries.

"That would be a 'small' in America," Gaz told me with a kind of sneering nostalgia, remembering the Pepsi-Colas of Pasadena where he had been, it turned out, with the Venture Scouts. He put some chips in his mouth. "What you've got there would be a 'small'." He brightened up. "You get to the bottom of it there and it's *full of ice.*"

Teenagers, out for an afternoon in the car in their tight clean jeans and striped cotton tops, eyed his burnt arms nervously. Old people walked past, pretending to ignore us but carefully avoiding our feet. "Closed," they murmured, staring numbly straight ahead. "Closed." The caravans rolled south along the motorway, full of children and dogs. Little Asian girls with great laughing eyes and white teeth caught sight of our bruised and chalky hands and immediately became thoughtful: the women, in paper-thin lamé trousers, hurried them past.

"Another hole in me shirt," said Gaz. "What a fucking sight I look."

We ate our chips and even threw a few of them at one another in a sort of desultory slow motion, while the teenagers looked on, prim, embarrassed.

Gaz walked off to the car.

"I'm sick of being stared at now," he said.

So we went, as he put it, arseholing down the M6 with the radio turned up full: AC/DC, Kate Bush, Bowie's "Station to Station" already a nostalgia number. How many times, coming back after a hard day like that, has there seemed to be something utterly significant in the curve of a cooling tower, or the way a field between two factories, reddened in the evening light, rises to meet the locks on a disused canal? Motorway bridges, smoke, spires, glow in the sun: it is a kind of psychic illumination. The music is immanent in the light, the day immanent in the music: life in the day. It is to do with being alive, but I am never sure how. Ever since Gaz had fallen off into the sea I had felt an overpowering, almost hallucinogenic sense of happiness, which this time lasted as far as Bolton.

Gaz never simply threw a rope down a crag; he "cobbed it off the top". He didn't fall: he "boned off". If the moves on a climb demanded as well as strength or delicacy that kind of concentration which leaves you brutalised and debilitated when you have done the moves, he called them "poiky". "That was a bit bleeding poiky," he'd say, hauling himself desperately over the top and trying to control the tremor in his left leg. "Fuck me." He soon recovered though. "A bazzer that. A bloody *bazzing* route!" He had made up some of these words himself. Others, like "rumpelstiltskin", which he used to mean anyone eccentric or incompetent, he had modified to his own use.

I saw a picture of him when he was a baby.

His parents kept it on the sideboard at home by the clock with the brass pendulum and the long chains. It was in a wine-coloured cardboard frame with gold edging and in it he looked older than his own father.

One Sunday we were sitting in a steep gully at Tissington Spires. It had been sunny all the way down in the car. Now if you looked into Dovedale you could see a feeble light bleaching out the moss and stones. The water was a gelid blue-grey colour in its deepest stretches; above it tumbled bleak slopes or rubble, destabilised by tree-felling and littered with huge raw logs; two or three anxious sheep stood between the river and the rock.

Loose stones trickled down the gully. It was as cold as a bus shelter in the centre of Leeds on a Friday night, and as crowded, with climbers standing or sitting awkwardly wherever roots or dead branches crossed the steep dusty slope. Their quiet voices came back from the rock. When a few specks of rain blew through the ruined trees, a shaven-headed boy looked up and laughed; then down at the purple tape in his hand, his neck bent in the attitude of the inmate of a camp.

There was a woman with one of the teams further down the gully, where a lot of dead wood had made it easier to find somewhere to sit. She had blond hair cut in an exact fringe above her eyebrows. Gaz, waiting in the queue for his turn at Yew Tree Wall, stared at her idly, biting the hard skin round his fingernails. She was belaying a climber on the wall. She fed him some rope, took it back in, running it deftly through the Sticht plate. He swapped feet uneasily on a sloping hold and asked himself, "I wonder if I'm supposed to be able to reach that? Apparently not." He tried again, slithered back to his original position. "You bastard." The minute figures of tourists by the river, catching the clatter of his equipment, shaded their eyes helplessly and tried to see if anything had happened. The girl looked up at him and when he still didn't make the move shivered with a mixture of boredom and cold.

She tried to pull the sleeves of her long sweater down over her wrists; smiled quickly at nothing, as if she was practising the expression. The boy with the shaved head wanted to take a photograph of her but she wouldn't co-operate. "Come on now. Big grin. Big cheesy grin." She reminded me of someone but I couldn't remember who. When I told Gaz he nodded, still watching her.

"I've seen her about," he said. "I've seen her a few times at the Bradford wall too, on a Tuesday night, climbing in pink tights." He chuckled. "Not bad! I wonder if she's married? Eh?" And he ducked his head in her direction with a significance I wasn't sure I'd caught. I laughed.

"Would it make any difference to you?"

He looked away, so I left it.

"It's not a climber she reminds me of," I said.

On the crux of Yew Tree Wall, a yawning lean to the right from the tips of two fingers hooked into a knife-edged pocket, Gaz lost his balance and had to grab an old aid sling threaded into the rock.

"Well that's fucked that then," he said viciously. "Back to stuffing mince into plastic bags tomorrow."

60

We abseiled off the tree at the top.

"You drive fifty miles to do a route, wait two hours for a lot of pillocks to clear off it, then you pox it up by pulling on a piece of tat." All the way back along Dovedale to the car he was in a foul mood; in the pub at Wetton that night he looked round with hatred at the tourists.

"All these dossers," he said loudly. "What are they ever going to do with their lives?"

In country pubs like this there is always a plump boy with a brand new French tracksuit top from the Grattan catalogue sitting opposite you with a packet of vinegar flavoured crisps. At the back of the room bikers plan their outrages: they will have a fire at the camp site, drink tinned beer, tease a dog. A middle-aged man walks stiffly past — under his tweed sports coat he has a striped shirt, a coloured scarf tied like a neck brace.

"They come out here at the weekends . . . If they walk down Dovedale like the fucking Pickerton Ramblers they think they've had a big adventure. 'Ex*cews* me,'" he mimicked. "'Could a climber like that *reelly* fall off? I mean reelly *hurt* himself?'"

"Yew Tree Wall won't go away," I said. "You can come back to it any time. Next Saturday if you like."

"How do I know that? I might die. It might fall down. Anything might happen. I might drive me car into a wall and end up in a wheelchair." He drank his beer. "It ruins your whole weekend, something like that. All you've got to look forward to is another week of dirty water, your hands in fucking dirty water till they split. You want to try it, you do." He got up and went to the lavatory, his great height and lurching, hunch-shouldered walk making him look even more dejected.

"Been out doing some climbing then?" the fat boy asked. He offered me a crisp and when I took one sat forward companionably. "Rather you than me," he said. "I bet you've seen some accidents at that game."

In country pubs like this women from the nearby towns dressed to the nines eat steak sandwiches from a paper napkin, holding their hands delicately in front of them like a praying mantis, gold bangles dangling from thin wrists. It's their night out, and their feet must be killing them. Every so often they lean down and with a furtive but curiously graceful motion adjust a shoe which is nothing more than a few slim red leather straps. After you have been climbing all weekend this gives you a sharp sexual surprise. With their make-up and perfume, their white shoulders displayed suddenly as they turn to someone and laugh, they are like women from another planet. You watch covertly to see if they will betray themselves further; they never do.

On the way home Gaz had the air of someone watching himself clinically to see how late he dared leave his braking. It was a kind of bitter investigation of his own technique. Once he swerved into the opposite carriageway of the A515 and drove along it waiting for me to say something. In the dark car I couldn't make out his expression. He said,

"Who did that girl at Tissington remind you of, if it wasn't a climber?"

"I can't remember."

At that time of Gaz's life driving and climbing were like two aspects or definitions of the same thing. Cars stood for the wish, climbing for the act.

I think of him showing off on a Saturday morning in the scattered early traffic of the B6106, or flirting with the tight little corners of the Strines Road on the way from Huddersfield to the climbers' cafes at Grindleford and Stoney Middleton:

The brickworks lurch past on one side, on the other white faces peer at us momentarily through the streaming windscreen of a Land Rover. The roads are still plastered with last year's orange leaves. Stone walls, sodden verges, sudden drops assemble themselves out of the mist only so Gaz can annihilate them; junctions and old gates yawn out at us and are snatched away. The Vauxhall rocks and dips as he forces it into bends fringed with dripping oaks and tilted white signposts. Everything is fog and wet, everything is at the wrong angle, after every narrow squeak he gives me a sidelong glance I pretend not to see. At Bole Edge, where the dark feathery conifers close in over the road, the mist thins without warning: *An old man on a bicycle* is silhouetted at the top of the hill, wobbling along against the bright morning sun!

Something else danced one Saturday among the heat mirages in the middle of the road.

"Did you see that? It was a hare! It was a bloody big hare!"

"It was only a bit of newspaper."

Later the reflection of my watch flickered on the dashboard; the limestone factories swam like casinos and amusement palaces in a golden haze; trapped in the obsessional net of drystone wall on the long sweeping rises by the A623 east of Buxton, groups of beech trees caught fire suddenly in the sunshine. Gaz accelerated. It was like being in a video game.

Though he made a considerable impression on me, I didn't actually see a great deal of Gaz. I was out with Normal a lot of the time; Gaz climbed mostly with Sankey.

Sankey was always so cautious and indirect, so ready to defer to your opinion. He wondered casually if you had a couple of days free that week: he knew full well you were on the dole. With him everything was open to negotiation. If, driving to a cliff he had known all his life, you asked, "Do we turn right here?", he would consider for a moment and then say, "Yes, yes, you can. Or of course you can go up round Ilkley if you want to. It's sometimes quicker that way." And when you stared at him: "Well it probably is further to go. But now you *can* get on to the A650, some people do prefer that way —"

By then you had missed your turning.

This drove Gaz mad, and he wouldn't have Sankey in the front seat of the Vauxhall with him. They got on all right in Sankey's car, a three-wheeler van about which he was very defensive. To improve its fuel consumption even further he had taken the passenger seat out, so that you sat in the back in the dark with the ropes and piles of equipment. They took me to Almscliffe in it one day: it bumped and banged along the Yeadon by-pass, rocking from side to side. "I'm going to puke up!" shouted Gaz. He gave me a wink. "I keep thinking, what if we get a puncture in the front wheel? I mean, you've only got the one, haven't you?"

Sankey screwed himself round in the driver's seat.

"They're very safe, these," he said. "Very safe cars."

Horns blared at him from the approaching traffic, into whose lane he had wobbled. For a moment all we could see of him was his elbows jerking about in silhouette as he sawed at the steering wheel. Gaz clutched himself among the rucksacks; it was an old joke, you could see, but a good one.

At Almscliffe you can't get out of the wind. It hisses in the greenish cracks and flutings. It blows from all directions at once even on a summer day. The dust gets into your eyes as you pick your way down the cold dark gullies that dissect the main mass of rock, while all around you Lower Wharfedale spreads its legs in the sunshine — farmland, spires, viaducts, hedges and trees. It might be a landscape much further south, much earlier in the year, great swags of blossom at the edge of every field. But up on the horizon the power-stations lie hull-down in ambush among the East Yorkshire coal pits.

Gaz got straight into his harness and on to the rock.

"I'm scared!" he complained after he had hand-jammed about forty feet up into the wind. He was just passing a thing like a melted, dripping end of an old candle. The crack he was climbing arrowed above him into the blue sky. Soon he would get his foot stuck in it.

Being there is like watching an old elephant, dying split-skinned in its own tremendous ammoniacal reek, gazing patiently back at you in a zoo. It hasn't moved for a long time, you judge, but you can still detect the tremor of its breath — or is it your own? Meanwhile the children shout and try to wake it up with buns. At Almscliffe the visitors walk about bemusedly, shading their eyes, wondering perhaps why the zoo-keeper has let them in on such a tragic occasion. They are generally middle-class people, careful not to drop their sandwich papers from the top. The crag bears them up passively, while bits of route description, boasts and obscenities circle round them on the wind.

"No you go left there and then swing round again."

". . . Syrett . . . Pasquill . . ."

"Go left from where you are!"

". . . Black Wall Eliminate in the rain, nowhere to rest, that fucking bog waiting for you underneath . . ."

"Left! You go *left* you maniac. Oh fuck, look at that."

This has never been a quiet place. It was the first of the great outdoor climbing walls, the model of a local crag. Its enthusiasts — parochial, cliqueish, contemptuous of the performance of outsiders and resentful of their cheery unconcern for precedent — believe that the sport was invented here. Generations of them have brought the rock to a high polish, like the stuff that faces the Halifax Building Society. Every evening local men — Yorkshire men, who hardly ever speak — do the low-level traverses until they learn to allow for the shine of the footholds, the flare and brutality of the cracks. Their arms and shoulders grow strong. Their clothes fray. They develop a slow way of looking at you. Down Wharfedale they have wives and kiddies and bicycles just like anyone else, but all they think about is which one of them will solve the last Great Problem.

It won't be Gaz, anyway.

In his orange-dyed karate trousers, with his runners jangling and clanging mournfully, he gingerly unlocked his foot. "What grade is this? Rubbish!" Fucking and blinding he made his careful way up: pulled in a few feet of rope: vanished somewhere among the bottomless clefts and queer boulders of the summit, where pic-nickers looked at him like owls. After a moment his head popped back over the top. "Come on! Never mind sitting on your arses down there, get some climbing done!"

As he brought me up he dangled his legs over the top like Pinocchio and stared out over the plain towards York, where the tourists would be making their way from shop to shop in a muzzy, good-tempered dream. He was in one himself. "You want to jam that crack mate," I heard him advise someone on another climb, "not layback it." After a moment he kicked his legs disconnectedly and sang in a maudlin voice, "I don't know what to do when you disappear from view . . ." Soon a great loop of rope hung down in front of me.

"For Christ's sake Gaz pay attention. Take in. Take in! If I fucking fall off —"

"You're not going to. Stay steady. Steady. You're all right. Can you get your hands in the break? Just stay steady and you'll do it," he said. "It's easy." He took the rope in tight anyway. "Look," he said, leaning out at an odd angle against his belays so that he could see down the climb; it made him look as if he had been photographed in the act of throwing himself off. "See there? Just above that bit of a rib there? . . . No *there*, above you, you wollock! . . . That's it, just there. Can you see a tiny little lay-off?"

I said I could.

"Well don't use that, it's no good."

The sun came down and scraped into the irregular corners like Gaz's mother scraping an oven. He moved his shoulders uneasily and exchanged his pullover for a T-shirt with a design advertising a northern equipment firm: "Troll Gets You High".

We had something to eat. Then, forced into inhuman, expressionistic postures by its grim logic, Sankey strained and contorted up Wall of Horrors, until his impetus ran out just under the crux. He stretched up: nothing. He tried facing left, then right, grinding his cheek into the gritstone. His legs began to tremble. All the lines on the rock moved towards him, in a fixed vortex. When he lurched suddenly on his footholds everyone looked up: he was only sorting through the stuff on his rack for something to protect his next two moves. If he took too long to find and place it he would come off anyway. His last runner was lodged in a crack like a section through a fall pipe, fifteen or twenty feet below him.

"Can you get something there?"

"Can you get anything in higher up?"

He didn't hear us.

He was fiddling about in a rounded break, his eyes inturned and panicky, his head and upper body squashed up as if he was demonstrating the limits of some box invisible to anyone else. Under the impact of fear, concentration, physical effort, his face went lax and shocked, his age began to show. By 1970 he had climbed all over the world; he had done every major route in Britain; the 'new' climbs were his only hope — violent, kinaesthetic, stripped of all aid. "Wall of Horrors!" he would say. "John Hart talked me up that, move by move, first time I led it. Years ago. It overfaced people then. Ha ha." He was forty, perhaps forty-five. As I watched him I wondered what he was doing it to himself for.

All the time Gaz was watching him too.

He had to predict when Sankey would go. He had to mother him.

The runner in the fall pipe was too close to the ground to be much good: if Sankey boned off, could Gaz run back far enough quick enough to shorten the rope? I didn't think he could. He fidgeted it backwards and forwards through the Sticht plate, which clicked and rattled nervously.

Up in his invisible box Sankey twisted one arm behind his back to get his hand into his chalk bag. His shadow moved uneasily on the buttress over to his left, the shadow of the rope blowing out behind it. Chalk smoked off into the turbulence as he shifted his feet.

The sun went in.

"OK, kid," he said. "Watch the rope."

Suddenly we saw that he was calm and thoughtful again. He stood up straight and went quickly to the top, reaching, rocking elegantly to one side, stepping up.

Things have moved on now, of course, but Wall of Horrors was still a test-piece then. When he came down several people were waiting to congratulate him. Most of them were boys of fourteen or fifteen who would one day solo it; against that time they were willing to give him uncontrolled admiration. They were dressed in white canvas trousers, sweatshirts and pullovers with broad stripes, in imitation of the American and Australian climbers whose pictures they saw in the magazines; in two or three years they would be wearing silkskin dance tights, courting anorexia in search of a high power-weight ratio, exchanging the magic words of European-style climbing: "screamer", "redpoint", "Martin Atkinson".

One of them said, "Are you Stevie Smith? I've seen you climb before, haven't I?"

Sankey gave his nervous laugh.

"No," he said.

He sat down tiredly among some boulders and began sorting through his equipment, strewing orange tape slings about in the dust as if looking for something that had let him down. Then he just sat, absentmindedly clicking the gate of a snaplink until Gaz brought him some coffee from a flask. As we walked away from the cliff the backs of my hands smarted in the wind. I saw the shadow of a dove flicker over the rock in the warm slanting light. These birds live in the high breaks and caves. They ruffle their feathers uncertainly, hunch up, explode without warning over your head; they come back in the evening. Sankey's eyes were losing the empty, exhausted look that had entered them on the wall.

On the way home Gaz said, "I wouldn't mind being an owl in my next life." Then he said, "I'm getting married next month." He had to shout to make himself heard over the engine of the three-wheeler.

I didn't go to the wedding — something intervened — but I needn't have worried, because Normal told me about it later.

"You should have been there," he said. "All the lads were there. What a send-off! And after they'd gone we went over to Running Hill Pits in Sankey's car and *climbed a route*. In our penguin suits!"

He showed me a photograph he had taken of Sankey nearing the top of a climb called Plum Line, in a hired morning suit and polished black shoes. From what I could make out Sankey had tied on to the rope with a couple of turns round his waist. His face was a white smear. Runners hung out of his trouser pockets.

"We were pissed out of our minds!"

Normal shook his head reminiscently as I leafed through the rest of the prints. They were all blurred: Gaz, with an appalled grin like an expressionist self-portrait, standing as if he had one leg shorter than the other; Normal himself, holding up a glass of beer and a chalk bag; someone I didn't recognise looking back over his shoulder as he came out of a door marked 'Men'.

"We shook chalk over them instead of rice. We were well pissed!"

"You didn't take any of his wife," I said. "I'd like to have seen her."

"She's very nice," said Normal sentimentally. "Very nice. They went to the Isle of Man, she'll enjoy that."

That night Sankey rang me up.

"I wondered if you were going out with Normal in the week?" he said.

"I'm not sure," I answered. "You know Normal."

"Only that I thought we could go to Millstone," he said cautiously, "and do Time for Tea. If you feel like it. If you've got nothing else on."

*

68

I lost touch with Gaz, although I had a postcard from him on his honeymoon at Douglas, and another one about six months later from the Verdon Gorge in Provence, which said in deeply-indented block letters, WELL HERE WE ARE IN VERDON, WEATHER IS WICKED KEEPS SNOWING, HARRY & DAVE GOT BENIGHTED 300FT FROM THE TOP THEY HAD TO SLEEP IN A TREE THE FIRST DAY. THE ROCK IS INCREDIBLE POSTCARD DOESN'T DO IT JUSTICE. SEE YOU GAZ. (I didn't know who Harry and Dave were but the Défile des Cavaliers, with its luxuriant vegetation and slightly pink limestone, looked nice: it might have been Symonds Yat, or Trow Gill in Yorkshire, but I suppose that was an effect of scale.)

I met him again by accident in Lodge's supermarket one Saturday morning about three years after the wedding. He didn't seem to have changed. His wife was with him, a short girl in dungarees, with one breast noticeably larger than the other and long hair which she pushed back continually from her face. She put her arms round his waist from behind and rubbed her cheek against his back. They had a toddler which sat in its pushchair watching them silently.

"Fucking hell," Gaz said to me. "I'll always remember you leading that — what was it! — Wall of Horrors. Wall of Horrors, what a name! Poiky stuff!"

"That was Sankey," I reminded him. For some reason I felt flattered anyway. "Wall of Horrors is a bit strong for me."

"You don't want to do yourself down," Gaz told me. "You were always a good climber. You just needed that bit of steadiness."

After they had done their shopping, they said, why didn't we go upstairs where you could have a cup of tea? That was what they usually did. Gaz paid, and his wife insisted we have cakes. They gave the little boy a drink of something bright red, but he couldn't seem to manage the glass well, and he didn't take much interest in it. He seemed bemused. The clatter, the steam, the Saturday-morning laughter made him blink. Gaz looked out of the window at the phone boxes in the square. "Same old place," he said with his typical grin. He still worked at the butcher's: I wouldn't have seen him there because he still worked in the back. He winked. "Still fetching the green tags out!"

When I thanked him for his postcard he said, "Verdon! Oh it was fucking great. Thousands of feet of limestone, 5b and 5c pitches all the way. Ron Fawcett had just been there, freeing a bolt ladder seven hundred feet up: it went at 7b, so they all said. 7b! Can you believe that as a grade? I can't. Dave was so freaked out he couldn't even *second* some of the pitches. We had to pull him up on the rope like a sack: he didn't know how to prusik!" He laughed and pushed his cup away. "Six run-outs of 6a, and no dinner all day, then you have to lead at 7b! Fucking appalling!"

A waitress came over and said to his wife, "I forgot to give you a spoon for your tart, love."

Gaz stared uncomprehendingly after her as she walked off. "Fucking bazzing!" he said less certainly, as if he remembered his enthusiasm but had forgotten what he was talking about. He got up to fetch us all another cup of tea. Over the noise of the woman at the next table his wife said, "I always tell him I wish he'd go out climbing more. He does love it. But he likes to be with the kiddy at weekends. They do, don't they?"

The child was a sad little thing. Its hair stood on end, much like Gaz's, and it was hard to tell whether it would smile at you or cry. When she saw me trying to attract its attention she said complacently, "Tired out, the poor little mite." She chuckled. "He gave me a fright this morning," she said, leaning forward and lowering her voice. "You'll never believe what he did." She had got up, she told me, at five in the morning, to find that it had stuck elastoplast dressings on the limbs of its soft toys and immured them in the nine-inch gap between the double glazing panes. "I don't know what he thought he was doing, do you?" She offered the child its drink, and it stared at her.

"Mind you," she went on, "don't you find you're so pleased at what you've got that you don't really care how they turn out? I mean, if he's just average that'll suit me. People tell me he should be taking a bit more notice now, but I say you're only a kiddy once, aren't you? Let him be a kiddy for a bit, eh?"

Over her shoulder I could see the phone boxes in the square. Up on the steeply terraced streets above them a man had locked himself out of his house. He walked to and fro outside it for a minute or two, threw himself violently against the front door. Nothing. He

70

knocked on a neighbouring door. Nothing there. He looked round warily then flung himself at his own front door again. He was so far away that everything he did had a kind of jerky, miniaturised savagery and motivelessness. Eventually he walked off rubbing his shoulder. A few spots of rain came down.

"I haven't got any of my own," I said.

8 · GETTING OUT

Before his marriage I often called for Gaz at the back door of the butcher's, at quarter past twelve, dinner time. All I ever saw in there was a dozen large pork pies neatly stacked in wire delivery trays; someone's racing bike propped up against a spotless wall. Gaz liked you to think his job was a bloodbath, but if you asked, "What do you actually do in there?" he would only wink and — flicking a cube of raw meat, dark red and speckled with yellow sawdust, off his jeans — grumble, "Bugger all most days. Mind you, I bust one of the machines this morning."

I wanted to know what the hooks in the ceiling were for. They slid on rails and looked as if they would bear quite heavy loads. He scratched his head. "Oh, this and that. Generally we hang stuff from them."

Staring into the pet-shop window at a sort of expanding plastic maze he said, "Me sister's got one of those. I never see what she keeps in it. It's always asleep when I get home. I know she keeps something in it but I've never seen it." And then, looking slyly at me, "I wonder if you can *eat* it — ?" Whatever he did at the butcher's was only tenable as a nightmare — sheep's eyes in the beer, plastic tags slit from lambs' ears, quartered hamsters. With an unguarded comment he might show it up, to himself as much as anybody, as boredom and drudgery. "I've gone right through these clogs. I'll

71

have to get new," he said as we sat on a bench in the sun. He unwrapped his sandwiches and opened one. "Fucking hell. Banana again."

Bob Almanac, oddly enough, was a teacher.

He taught at a comprehensive in Lockwood and already had a smattering of Urdu. "I only went into it for the long holidays. In the Sixties everyone wanted you to have a career. That was the big thing then, a career." He enjoyed reading *The Lord of the Rings* to the kids; one or two of them seemed interested. At college he had grown his hair down to his shoulders. It was hard for him to understand why they wanted theirs short, or why they fought with such insistent brutality among themselves. "Kids'll always fight, I know that. But this seems so systematic." He said he sometimes found himself bellowing at children in the street, "I'll sort you out if you keep on doing that!" It was out of proportion.

A climber called Mick had a job at the pipeworks, a sixty acre desert over towards the M62, tunnel kilns buried in the hillside like air-raid shelters, chimneys against the sky, stack after stack of earthenware pipes in the rain. Bleak looking houses had been built at the edge of it according to some patent system from the Fifties, not even of local stone. All day he smashed up faulty pipes with a spade, or swept the factory floors. When he got bored he tinkered with the sweeping machine until its performance grew erratic; he fell off it and broke his thumb. Sometimes when he had nothing to do at all he would fill a wheelbarrow with clay and pour water on it, then spend the afternoon throwing fragments of pipe into the mud, dreaming over a kind of miniature, internalised Passchendaele. When they gave him one of the bigger pipes to break up he kept it back until he thought of a new way of doing it; sometimes he saved it all day. He might, if no one was looking, run the sweeping machine into it, or trundle it into a pile of other pipes. "Once," he said, "I karate-kicked one of the cunts into six pieces." He nodded. "Six fucking pieces," he repeated, giving every word a heavy emphasis. "What do you think of that?"

The pipeworks had won some annual award to industry ("The fuckers 'ave invented a *straight pipe*," Mick told us) and his supervisor said to him: "Give it a really good do, Mick, then vanish.

You know. Go behind a machine. We want the visitors to think it's always this clean."

"I knew it were that as soon as he opened his mouth," Mick claimed with deep satisfaction. "I knew it were going to be that the second he opened it. Good enough to sweep the cunting floors but not to meet the cunting Royals. What a crock of shit."

He was an assistant team-leader in the local mountain rescue.

After school he had gone directly into an apprenticeship as a garage mechanic. Within seven months the garage had bankrupted itself and no one else would take an apprentice on. "They were all shit-scared of going bump themselves by then. Everyone were going down like ninepins." Whenever we went past the pipeworks in someone else's car, Mick would scream and fart and make machine-gun noises, writhing about in the back seat to indicate hits. "My apprenticeship. What a fucking crock of shit that was."

Besides working on the railway and in High Adventure, Normal had been what he called a 'silver service' waiter. He hadn't lasted long at it, he admitted; though when he wanted to he could take on an impressively servile tone.

Climbing, Bob Almanac believed, had it in common with escapology that while its dangers were artificial they were perfectly real. The hinge between the game and its consequences was an act of choice. You were not compelled by the circumstances of an ordinary life to accept the straitjacket, the lengths of stainless steel chain or the padlocked sack: but once you had, and they had shut the coffin lid on you and dropped you in the River Thames, there was only your own technique and nerve between you and suffocation.

"The river's as real as you like," he would repeat with a shiver. "As real as you like. I admire those blokes. I do."

He didn't think it had anything in common with Russian roulette.

Saturday night above the Milnsbridge Liberal Club: a bar and disco in three rooms papered with neutral wood-chip. Though they had the windows wide, and fire-extinguishers propping the doors open, the air was still hot; it had a thick powdery taste of perfumes and deodorant. Some fat women were sitting in a line in the middle

73

of the floor making boat-rowing motions and singing along with the disco, "hang on, hang on to what we've got," while their youngest — boys awkward in brand new jeans, spoiled girls wearing orange lipstick and white dresses which made their skinny shoulders look for a moment mature and creamy in the dim light — watched in furious silence from tables pushed back to the walls.

"It's only a bit of a do," Mick from the pipeworks explained to me: a bit of fund-raising for the rescue team. "Most of them are here now, you can see them stood at the bar." They'd dance with their wives if the shop-talk faltered, otherwise it was Dark Mild and the Bell stretcher. "Oh, and it's Paul's twenty-first, too. His Mum's here. Nice trousers Paul. Nice shirt."

"Fuck off."

"Paul's mum helped us out with the caterer's."

Paul was showing off to some of his cousins, who had come over from Barnsley in a Ford Escort. "It only makes sense to get your casualty *down*," he advised them in a loud voice. "OK, so he's got a broken back. So what? You might make it worse. You might kill him. But how can anyone even put a bandage to him if he's hanging off a rope?"

He saw the rest of the team looking on ironically.

"You wouldn't bandage a broken back of course," he said.

There was a silence, into which he laughed rather wildly.

To help him out, Mick, very much the team-leader, said, "I can see the sense in that." Then he shrugged and gave a wide grin. "But look Paul, if you keep your mouth shut we shan't have fuckers falling down it all the time, shall we?" During the laughter at this — in which Paul joined — Mick went out to dance. The fat women wouldn't have anything to do with him, so he capered about on his own for a bit, heaving and dragging himself across the floor like a sack of coal, eyes inturned, forehead dripping, feet thudding and banging arhythmically. When he came back he said, "This is why people generally get pissed at these affairs. Nowt else to do."

He hit himself on the forehead.

"Oh fuck, I've got me MRC Syllabus coming up tomorrow. Why didn't anyone remind me? Ask me summat, for Christ's sake! No wait, I know. Paradoxical respiration! Only occurs from a flail segment of rib. You can't — no don't *tell* me, you dozy crock of shit! — you can't stop it going in, so stop it going out. OK? Right. Now, in classic pneumothorax . . . no, tension pneumothorax . . ."

He shook his head impatiently.

"I've forgotten that fucker's name," he admitted. "Anyway, your heart and everything get pushed into your other lung . . . Treatment: avoid morphine and bang a wide-bore hypodermic needle straight into the pumped-up lung: you can control the air-flow with the end of your finger."

"What about mediastinal flap?" someone suggested to him.

He was puzzled for a minute. "Now that's nearly the same," he said. He thought. "But you'll get that with *penetrating* wounds," he remembered triumphantly. "An ice axe or summat. That's the example they always give. Some incompetent fucker falls on his ice axe, you see, at the top of Market Street . . . Where's the bog here?"

He wandered off to find it.

Sankey, who had once been on the team himself, laughed. "He'll drink fourteen pints of beer now and wonder why he can't remember anything in the morning. He was an idiot even before they got him in the pipeworks."

"Will he pass the exam?" I asked.

"Oh aye kid. He'll pass it."

"Bowel sounds'll be the same whether it's spleen or liver," I heard someone point out: "They both give diminished or absent bowel sounds."

Sankey told me about a friend of his who had had a steel plate put in his leg as a result of a skiing accident. When he fell off a climb a year or two after the operation he smashed his ankle to a pulp.

"The plate's rigid, you see," Sankey explained, "so your leg has to give somewhere else. He packed it in after that." He was silent for a moment, then he added:

"He can still walk a bit."

Later on, to get away from the disco, Sankey, Mick and I went next door, where the caterers had the food spread out on folding tables. There wasn't much left now, and they were beginning to pack it up, but among the bits of pinkish ham and half-empty trifle cases, Mick found some little cakes iced in pastel colours — violet, yellow, a strange luminous green — and decorated with bits of crystallised peel. While we were eating them Paul's mother, who was about fifty, walked in tiredly, sighed, and sat down to look at the cars parked solid along the street. "There's no air in here," she said, as if she was talking to an empty room. After a minute or two she blew her nose, patted her hair. "I can see you two gannets are enjoying yourselves in the usual way," she said to Mick and Sankey. Mick went over to her.

"Are yer all right?"

"Aye, I am, but I've had enough."

"Well, I'm not surprised."

"I'm phoning them up in the morning. I just haven't been satisfied."

She went out and came back again with a florist's bouquet wrapped in cellophane. It looked like one of the cakes.

"Have you seen *this*?"

Sankey wanted to know if I was getting out much with Normal. Because — giving me an oblique look — if I wasn't he could easily start picking me up at weekends. There was plenty of room in the back of the van. "If you weren't getting out, kid, only if you weren't getting out." It would split the cost of the petrol, too.

"I can see the sense of that."

9 · WIVES

In fact, I wasn't getting out much with Normal.

During May and June the weather had improved steadily. Along the edges of the gritstone moor, clematis grew on every cottage, insects hummed in the laburnum. As soon as the flowering cherry was finished, ornamental broom and rowan began pouring across the lawns a scent sometimes so strong and confectionery it overpowered itself, like jasmine in a closed room. You knew you could smell something but not what it was. At six in the morning the villages were already lapped in hot brilliant air. By afternoon the limestone crags further south burned above their steep little valleys with the luminosity of exposed bone. Beneath them masses of hawthorn blossom were piled up like exotic buttercream, from which streamed downwind vanilla and corruption intertwined; and on the gently curving slopes above, a bewildering variety of flowers none of us could name. In the evenings the rock seemed to sweat from inside. As it grew dark the lupins in front of Sankey's house gave off like tall translucent candles a perfume so delicate it might have been mistaken for a faint white light.

If you had wanted to you could have climbed from five in the morning until ten at night: Normal, though, arranged to go out, turned up late, and under the pretext of looking for a piece of equipment, checking a guidebook or finding a picture of some new route in a magazine, took you to his house instead. There a lassitude overcame him. He made cups of instant coffee, leafed through the catalogues he still got through the post from contacts in the trade, and told you stories about himself: while you watched anxiously as the light slanted round the room towards mid-morning, interrupting when you could bear it no longer.

"I thought we were going to Cave Dale?"

Sometimes he just didn't turn up.

When he did get out he wanted to sit in the cafes as if it was still February, or look for his old friends and introduce you to them; now that the summer had come it was as if he didn't want it after all.

The heat reminded me of my last day in London.

I had been impatient to leave by then. I had been spending three weekends out of four on the sandstone outcrops in East Sussex: anything to get away from Camden Town where in summer the Irishmen sleep the day away in parks, their fat red shoulders covered with strips of peeling skin like shreds of Kleenex, and a skim of rubbish bobs companionably past on the Regent's Canal in the frying light — lumps of styrofoam packing like decayed heads, slivers of wood and soft-drink cans bound together with a creamy brown curd of detergent foam and oil. I had given up the keys to my flat. I felt contained but energetic, as if I only had to push with my arms to be somewhere else. When I went to say goodbye to Pauline, she was answering the telephone.

"We'd love to come," she said into it. "Yes. Yes, his name is Anthony. Didn't I tell you? He's from Guyana." She laughed. "Yes. Black. Very black indeed!" After a pause she said, "I'll bring him then. OK. Yes, it was time to meet someone older. I was so bored with all those boys —" She laughed again and put the phone down.

"Those bloody old women in Notting Hill," she said to me.

One of her cats jumped up on to the table in front of her. She sighed and rubbed its sandy belly, buried her face suddenly in its fur — "Oh, Rutherford you smell so wonderful! Hello Rutherford! Oh, hello!" — then stared at the books piled by the toaster and the empty plates: *Art and Act*, *Vision and Design* in a first edition, *Flemish Painters*. She touched the spine of the Roger Fry. Sunlight projected obliquely on the nylon carpet the image of the window frame behind her. One thick vertical bar crossed at three quarters of its length by a thinner, shorter one, both enclosed in a parallelogram of shadow: a strange figure, the dark part the colour of earth and lichen, the bright parts green and gold. All morning the sun had been forcing it round to the north. It elongated itself to escape. Eventually it would go too far and break to pieces against the shelves of books, but not before the cat Rutherford had got down in it and wriggled with pleasure.

"Let's have some tea," said Pauline. "I can easily make some!" she added, as if this ability had suddenly surprised and delighted her.

She went to the sink with the breakfast plates and a knife, then stopped there, kettle not yet offered to the tap, the strong light falling across her face and arms from the window like the light on a becalmed sail. She was looking out across the flat roof where she sometimes sat in the evening in one of two or three bleached kitchen chairs, listening to the traffic go up Camden High Street towards Hampstead. She would be, I thought, forty or forty-one that year. On the floor near her feet the cat tried to attract her attention by touching her ankle tentatively with one paw.

78

"Just look at this animal! Don't you wish you could feel like that? I mean really alive and *inside* yourself? Rutherford, I love you!"

Water banged in the pipes. She turned the tap off; on again; off.

"So!" she said. "Manchester! Oh, I hope you're going to be really successful there!"

I picked the cat up. It gazed impassively, then rolled out of my hands and back on to the floor. I had already seen that, to climbers, climbing was less a sport than an obsession. It was a metaphor by which they hoped to demonstrate something to themselves. And if this something was only the scale of their own emotional or social isolation, they needed — I believed then — nothing else. A growing familiarity with their language, which I had picked up by listening to them as they practised on the indoor wall in Holloway, and their litter, spread out on a Saturday afternoon like a glittering picnic in the deep soft sand at the foot of Harrison's Rocks, had already made me seem quite different to myself. Besides, I had done a fifty foot classic abseil down a piece of blue polypropylene rope, in shorts and a running shirt: if I needed reminding of that the burns were still there on my neck and thigh. How could you remain the same when you had stepped off the top backwards in that way, straight out into the air and into whatever was going to happen?

Quite soon I would meet Normal and begin to discover that this does not say all there is to say. Meanwhile the polypropylene — a material which will not take any kind of shock-load — glowed cheap, dangerous and colourful in a cupboard, and everyone I knew bored me. Their houses bored me and I showed it by doing two-finger pull-ups on the door frames. I felt as if I understood something about myself which Pauline would not now ever know. This made her appear vulnerable. For some reason I thought of that as a victory.

So I said, "On a Friday night you can catch a train from Manchester Piccadilly and be in Derbyshire in fifteen minutes. That's the only reason I'm going there. Oh, and you can get to Wales cheaper."

She looked down at the table.

"Even so," she said quietly, "I hope something happens for you there. The kettle won't take long."

The cat was scratching at the door.

*

79

I had hated Pauline when I first met her, in a dull cafe in the provinces. "Look," she had said then, "you have exactly what you like and I'll pay, OK? They've got something they call curd tart, oatcakes, all sorts of things."

With its wooden chairs just too small for adults and polished with use the place looked like the classroom of an old-fashioned infants' school from which the children had run away. A wallpaper of tiny red and brown flowers — poppies perhaps — obsessively curving into one another, gave an effect of stealth. On one side of the room they had renovated a Victorian fireplace with a convoluted patent back, then stuffed its grate with coloured tissue. From the window you could just catch sight of a cemetery on the slope of a hill.

"Curd tart is the 'specialte maison'!"

I laughed, and so did Pauline's shy young American friend with the steel-rimmed spectacles. She was out to entertain us, especially the American, but all her stories were about food and drink, or people who had put something over on one another, and I wondered what to make of her.

Her hair was scraped rawly back from her face and held in a bun with two plastic slides. She had on a pinkish T-shirt under which her breasts hung lumpily; a black cotton skirt; leather sandals from some Mediterranean visit. Her legs were bare, white with blue veins, and a little gooseflesbed. She had come to buy some of my father's books. That day I put her between forty-five and fifty, because though I hated the little cafe myself I resented her patronising it; and I thought for some reason she was the wife of a university lecturer. It wasn't until later that I saw how beautiful her jaw was, or how her face could become so suddenly still and tranquil.

"In fact," she said, "I got the Morris off him for twenty five pounds less than he asked. I left him sitting on the running board with his head in his hands!"

The American boy broke up a scone but didn't eat it.

"Why won't they let you read industrial architecture at Oxford?" he asked me. "Is it only snobbery?"

Pauline laughed.

"Or antiques!" she said. "Wouldn't that be lovely?"

I saw the American look at her blankly then rest his eyes deliberately on the wall above her head, where in the picture-glass of one of the paintings that hung there he could perhaps see reflected a wobbly image of the view outside: roofs and gable ends going up without perspective, stacked on top of one another at odd angles, filling the window so there was only a frieze of white sky at the top. He was eighteen or twenty but the spectacles often gave him a detached air which made him seem older. Next to his plate he had opened a book of Marianne North flower paintings.

"If you're interested in that kind of thing," I said to him, "I think you can take a canal trip through the town, to see the backs of the factories. It depends how long you're going to be here."

"Oh, it's much nicer to do that in France," said Pauline. "Two weeks in the Midi, with gourmet food and wine!"

"Very nice," said the American boy.

She got up immediately to pay.

"I wonder if they can tell us about toilets and things?" she said.

I met the American outside the lavatory a few minutes later. He smiled, his spectacles flashed shyly, and he stepped out of my way when there was no need to. From the lavatory you could hear the river; three days' rain rushing down off the moor. Some uncarpeted stone steps led down to a mirror on the landing. I stood looking at myself there, waiting for them to leave. I had already said goodbye. A quiet murmur came up from the cafe, then I heard Pauline say, "They change the library round once a month. You suddenly find yourself quite lost."

A spoon rang against the rim of a cup. In a quite different voice she said: "Strange. That's so strange. Are you coming, Martin?"

Afterwards I realised she had been nervous. "You stared all the time," she told me. "At both of us. Martin was nervous too." And once I began to visit her there I found she felt more comfortable in London. She lived in an untidy flat above the fruit market in Camden, and at weekends had her own stall up at Camden Lock, where she sold Victorian prints and secondhand books. I never saw Martin again.

"Some of my stuff is quite good," she said. "Modern firsts. You know."

She kept most of it in a fruit store, a place like a cave, cool and dark at the back, the door a square of dazzling sunshine through which you could see the railings in Stuley Place. Boxes of fruit went up to the whitewashed ceiling; against the wall leaned a broken ladder and two or three faded, neatly-rolled canvas awnings. Unbranded three-piece suits, in plastic bags to keep them smart, lay draped here and there over the boxes of Antonio Mazzani peaches and Tasmanian apples, like empty executive glove-puppets: the trader with whom Pauline shared the rent of the store sold them as a sideline, from under the artificial grass on his barrow. She was always knocking them on the floor.

She loved to sort through her stock, the peripheries of which sometimes merged in a fatal dreamy way with her own collection, absorbing editions she had replaced, novels she had outgrown long before she met me.

"Oh," she would say suddenly, as if she had walked into a wall. "This is one of mine."

It would be Leonard Woolf's *Growing*, or *The Hunters and the Hunted* by Sacheverell Sitwell — not so much reminders of as signals from another part of her life.

Moving the books about was surprisingly hard work. I went over there with her in the afternoons, ostensibly to help choose fresh stock for the weekend, trundle it over to the Lock on an old porter's trolley, and set up the stall; but really so that I could watch her move tranquilly from box to box, packing and unpacking them. The air was warm and full of the slightly sour smell apples have even when they are perfectly sound. Light flared in from the street outside. There was always a muffled banging from the building next door, as of masonry being chiselled away: distant, rhythmic, self-absorbed. Pigeons nodded and bobbed among the squashed fruit near the door, cooing hypnotically. I leafed through the books she offered me, looking for signs of her personality; or stirred with my foot the boxwood splinters, the discarded tangerine wrappers — blue tissue paper with a bright yellow sticker — on the dusty concrete.

"Let me see . . . shall I sort out some paperbacks now, do you think? Oh look, *Nostromo*! I bought this in Ontario. Ontario! I'm not saying how many years ago that was."

She was less interested in the books than the dates she found pencilled in them, the inscriptions and marginal comments, the yellowed newspaper articles that fell from between their pages.

"I never got past page sixty-three," she said, showing me the corner of that page, still folded down. "My writing in those days! Horrible! Shall we sell it or keep it?"

"Sell it."

There was a barred window high up in one wall of the store, looking out over an overgrown privet bush and a yellowish-grey brick wall. The boxes underneath it were always damp: every week we would find two or three books which had developed a thick white mould. These we threw on the pile of rubbish — lemonade cans, chicken bones, cigarette cartons and black dustbin bags — which gathered daily in a corner of the wall by the doorway of Fishon Gowns on the other side of the road. Pauline called it 'The Graveyard'. Every time you went out with something, pigeons walked purposefully over to see what you had; while others, sick and blackened-looking in the sun on top of the old air-raid shelter at the junction with Buck Street, stared down without interest. The buzz of a sewing machine came from the clothiers.

Pauline held out a copy of *Nothing* by Henry Green.

"I decided to save this."

At night after the pubs and dance halls had closed people ran down Inverness Street smashing bottles and shouting. Pauline would touch the side of my face. "Don't you ever find yourself frightened?" But she would never say of what. Her body looked white and strange to me in the sodium light that leaked round the edges of the curtains, browning the bedclothes and glittering off the old fashioned Coca-Cola bottle she kept on a shelf. I had revised my opinion of her legs, her breasts; I thought she was probably thirty-five or thirty-six. The shouts of the market traders woke me before her in the mornings, and I rather missed that when we got married and moved further over towards Camden Road.

"I've already got a daughter," she told me two or three weeks before

83

the wedding. It wasn't so much a confession, I recognised, as a challenge. "I don't suppose it matters, does it? She's called Nina, and she lives with her grandmother, very happily, and I visit them every time I go up for a PBFA book fair. It's easy from Ilkley, and I can even manage Harrogate."

"I'm astonished."

"Oh, Nina and I are great friends."

Nina, I soon found, was about two and a half years old, with blonde hair cut in an exact neat fringe above her eyebrows. Outside the house she wore velour dresses in pink, or a pinny full of poppies; patent leather sandals and white ankle socks: but for her curiously mobile features and rather direct grey eyes she would have been what her grandmother called 'a proper little girl'. Inside, she dragged a plastic toy around the floor all day long on a length of yellow string. It made a desultory clicking sound and then more often than not fell over.

"Twisted!" she said. She looked at me and shrugged. "All gone!"

While I untangled it for her she lifted her arms in the air slowly. A series of indrawn expressions passed like grimaces over her face, which she turned upwards so that she appeared to be gazing into a corner of the ceiling: suddenly it split across the middle in a smile so wide and toothless, with her eyes so seamed and slitted-up above it, that it looked like an old woman's.

"Push me," she said ecstatically. "In the pushchair!"

"Nina, we don't need the amateur dramatics," Pauline told her.

Later, when Nina had gone to bed, the grandmother said, "Those dungarees are a bit tight on her, but I don't want to put her into ordinary trousers yet. It's another step in age, isn't it?" She smiled at me. "I hate to see them grow up," she said. "Don't you?"

Before she retired she had been a district nurse.

"Out came the stomach pump!" she would exclaim at breakfast. "*Down* went the saline. I kept thinking, 'How long? How long?' because after half an hour, you know, you're supposed to get them into Out Patients. But then — blork! — up it all came, twenty aspirins, enough for kidney failure." She illustrated this anecdote by nodding her head forward over the table and moving both hands rapidly away from her gaping mouth. "Blork! I was so relieved."

I liked her. She spoke of a 'sea fret', meaning a cold mist; she described herself as having to wait all morning at the butcher's, 'looking like cheese at fourpence'. In age, her face had become pouchy. Her heavy spectacles, blue-rinsed hair and full-lipped, slightly slack mouth had given her the almost middle-European look many older Yorkshirewomen have. She loved Nina, but it was clear that when she looked at her she was seeing other children. She greeted with delight each remembered way of laughing or standing, of refusing to do something, by staring absently down the neat rather bleak garden at the flowering privet with its drift of fallen petals the colour of turned brass. It might have been a sister or a cousin she was seeing, in another garden fifty years ago; it might have been a younger brother caught picking marguerite daisies as big as fried eggs and turning his head away to shout, "It wasn't me." She glimpsed their mannerisms intricated in every action. She watched the child each time it wept or waved goodbye — "Goodbye!" — as if she was trying to decode it .

"Is it you she sees," I asked Pauline, "when you were Nina's age?"

"You're kidding yourself," said Pauline briefly, "if you think that," and after our second or third visit told me, "I'd rather go there on my own really." She added by way of explanation, "I think we should all have private areas in our lives."

So I saw Nina less often than I might have. When Pauline was visiting I went to the cinema, or, left in charge of the books, mooned in the Winter Gardens, Ilkley. There on the collapsible shelving on either side of him, as he sat on his hard chair under the impressive gilt balconies, each dealer had his copies of Henry Williamson, Phil Drabble, *Mein Kampf, A Yorkshire Boyhood*. Storm Jameson was less popular than she had been. I got on with them perfectly well, though I found quite early that they knew nothing about the insides of books. There was always a bright strongly-smelling yellow stream in the urinal; while outside, Ilkley rested from its labours in the sunshine: comfortably-off, turned inward to face the past, old women on the benches, old men in cream cotton jackets, the scent of the fading stocks in the little parks.

(I got my dinner at the fish and chip bar, where you could sit

85

down, or American Style Eats. The life that goes on in cafes is domestic but minimal. Alone in one you pour your tea, unwrap a knife from a paper serviette that says 'Forte' or 'Thank you, we hope you will call again at Marie's'; there is as much comfort as you like to create out of the rattle of crocks or the slump of the waitress's shoulders, and no further claim on you as there would be at home.)

We did all four of us go to the swimming baths together one day, Rain dashed against the windows. Shrieks and shouts echoed back from the walls like the noises in a zoo, running together under the roof into a kind of undertone, a repetitive endless wailing. It was the hour of the afternoon reserved for the under-fives. The mothers glanced vacantly at one another above the heads of their children: little wet tails of hair lay on the brown napes of their necks. The babies milled slowly with their arms, rotating in the warm blue water. They stared at the flickering reflections; or, very close and without recognition, at a coloured ball floating on the surface of the water. Toddlers jumped in from the side — again — again! — while the attendant balanced on a step ladder in his grubby white shorts, tennis shoes and wet fawn socks, cleaning the windows. DEEP END, it said above him in huge block letters.

"Jump now Nina! Nina, jump!"

I sat on the bench provided for spectators, watching Pauline and her mother trying to persuade the girl to swim. Nina, though, clung to the steps and looked up and down the pool. "Nina! Nina!" they called encouragingly, but she wouldn't jump. Below her proper little nylon swimsuit, her legs looked white and waxy; grimaces replaced one another on her face. "Oh dear," said the grandmother. "Oh dear, what a baby." Pauline tried wading about with Nina in her arms, but even that was too close to the water, and she had to be put back on the steps. In the end she fell in from them, howling, and the grandmother tugged her about by the hands, reciting nursery rhymes.

Pauline, who had begun to look impatient, swam a length of the bath and then swung herself powerfully out of it at my feet. Immersion had brought the blue veins near the surface of her skin. "I can't stand any more of this," she said, walking off to get changed. "Let her drown!" She laughed down at the other women.

86

Light flickered up from the bottom of the pool.

I waited for them in the lobby with its pink-lilac walls and cold radiators, its machines for serving confectionery. Old fashioned fire extinguishers stood under the notice boards. "Don't touch anything Robert," said a woman's voice from the changing rooms. "Now don't touch." In the green gloom of a tank by the door, tiny ornamental fishes moved languorously, or flicked like knifeblades as they vanished among the bubbles and weeds. Pauline came out first.

"I know how Nina feels," I said. "I hated it at that age too."

She stared at me.

"Water," I said.

"What good will it do her to avoid things?"

Nina was always falling. When they took her to Whitby she fell in the sea. At Dainty Debbie's — where her grandmother took her once a week to buy velvet dungarees and blue plastic frogs to hold her hair in bunches at the sides of her head — the mole-like woman behind the counter asked her if she wanted to be an actress when she grew up, and she fell off a chair. She fell out of bed in the middle of the night and crawled about under it in a kind of confused rage looking for a way out, while the grandmother called, "Nina! Nina! Where are you?", imagining the child had somehow left the room. One evening, showing off before she went upstairs, she fell through the glass coffee table in the lounge. It broke into ten or a dozen pieces and one of them, about three inches long, went into the small of her back.

"I hate these places," said Pauline. "They can always find something wrong with you if they try."

We sat on the curved plastic chairs in the Royal Infirmary, drinking cups of coffee from a machine. Pauline had driven us up overnight in her old tinny Citroën. It was nine thirty and in the strong morning light everything already seemed to be too clean and sharp-edged. From one corridor you glimpsed another one like it at right angles — sun splashed across it to a notice and a yellow door opened on a tiled room. A figure walked past from right to left and then from left to right again. Off the waiting area, with its blue carpet, were other waiting areas where other women gazed expressionlessly at you from behind hatches and dispensary windows in a meaningless replication of space. I felt dizzy, and as if my skin was more sensitive than usual to the movements of the air.

We were there for an hour, while Pauline's mother tried to find out what was happening. Once or twice we thought we saw her wandering about with a docket in her hand. She had been waiting all night for news. She peeped into an open office, went in, and then came out again. "Well then, is that all right?" I heard her say, then, "But what's his name? Oh, I see." She went away slowly down the passage, her bulk and her off-white coat giving her for once a defeated air.

"I don't know how she manages," said Pauline. "I wouldn't know where to start."

An empty wheelchair was pushed past.

"There you are," she said, as if it contained a helpless patient only she could see. "You come in perfectly all right and go out wearing a neck brace."

She shivered.

"Are you cold?"

"No, I'm tired. It's that bloody little car."

Voices came from another corridor.

When Pauline's mother came back she said, "We'll just have to wait." For a moment as she stood in front of me I thought she was an orderly or a nurse. It was the pale coat. In a place like that even somebody you know can be mistaken for an official: you don't recognise them immediately, especially if they come from an unexpected direction. "We'll just have to be patient." She looked very discouraged. She settled herself heavily in one of the plastic chairs. She wouldn't have coffee from the machine; it was too strong. "I just think of her pulling that little aeroplane about on the floor," she said suddenly, as if she had been thinking about it all night, "when she should have been in bed."

"I can't wait here," said Pauline. "I can't bear it here another minute."

"She had us all wound round her little finger," the grandmother was saying as we got up. She called out after us, "I don't think it can be the spleen. The spleen would have gushed."

Outside the town, where the traffic signals were festooned against a lowering sky, the road climbed up between conifer plantation, through the odd prosperous village with its churchyard full of cedars, then over rough pasture and half-drained moorland. It was a curiously tiring landscape. Pauline drove for twenty minutes, slowly at first then faster. "I hate that expression," she said. "'Wrapped around her little finger'." She studied the road as if it puzzled her, narrowing her eyes momentarily at each bend. "Poor Nina." On top of the moor the car rocked in the wind; rusting tractors, canted over in trenches they had dug themselves, lay scattered over the bare, peaty slopes; the road began its steep descent into the Vale of York.

"There's a place to park here somewhere."

Five or six vehicles were already lined up in it. Children ran about between them, sheltered from the wind by a stone wall and a tuck in the farmland, while their parents had tea out of a flask or pointed back the way they had come at the road falling away into the valley. There was a man in one of the fields above flattening the grass at carefully chosen spots with heavy blows from the back of a spade; he stopped to massage the small of his back and watch two of the children hunting for grasshoppers.

"Here's one! I've got one!"

"There's one here! There's one here on a rock! Oh, I've killed it."

Their mother had a blue picnic stove going. While she tried to fill the kettle at a dried up stream that came out under the wall, her husband was kneeling on the gravel in his shorts looking through the driver's door of their home-painted maroon and yellow car. He went round to the boot and got out an old wind-up gramophone in beautiful condition, and with great care made it play 'Moonlight in Vermont', 'A Nightingale Sang in Berkeley Square', and something the chorus of which went,

> Someone's been polishing up the sun,
> Brushing up the clouds of grey —
> How did they know that's how I like it?
> Everything's going my way!

An old woman further down the row of cars seemed to enjoy this one. She smiled and waved, nodded her head in time, tapped her fingers on the arm of the folding chair they had put her out in; he waved back and played it twice more, while some pages torn from *Peaches* blew round his reddened ankles in the sun.

"Christ!" I said. "Look at them! Do you want to go somewhere else?"

Pauline, who had been watching them with an expression I couldn't interpret, laughed.

"They're only people," she said. She felt about in the glove compartment. "I had a comb in here somewhere but I think it's dropped down the back."

"I really think we ought to be at the hospital. Your mother's on her own."

She got out of the car and slammed the door.

"I *thought* you weren't saying much!" she shouted in at me, with her face up close to the glass.

We went back to London by train a few days later. Pauline didn't want to drive. The weather was hot, the local connection dark and noisy, clogged with air that had been breathed before. At Leeds a bald man catching the same Inter-City 125 dropped his spectacles on the platform at our feet.

All the way down to London, immense columns of smoke rose from the burning stubble in the fields. Near at hand they were a thick greyish white; on the horizon, faint, brown, dissipated smears through which the late sun burned like a blood orange. Misty lenses and feathers drifted over the dark stripe of woodland, the flint churches and comfortable houses between Newark and Peterborough. A little further south Pauline counted twelve plumes of smoke. "You can see the flames now!" But the other passengers seemed not to care. The carriage was almost empty anyway: a family two or three seats away played cards quietly; whenever the train slowed, the man who had dropped his spectacles walked irritably up and down the aisle or complained about the chill of the air conditioning.

Near Peterborough in the twilight, everything became fluid, deceptive: a charred field with small white puffs of smoke hanging just above the ground revealed itself as a long sheet of black water, fringed with reeds and dotted with swans; even the stubble, burning in the middle distance like a line of liquid fire, sometimes resolved into the neon signs of factories and cinemas. It was soon dark. I went to the buffet, and when I came back Pauline asked me,

"Doesn't it break your heart to see anything so beautiful?"

Then she was quiet again until we got closer to London and she noticed a long row of lights saying STEVENAGE, STEVENAGE in the night.

A month or two later she sold the Citroën; and not long after that got the chance to move back into her old flat. "It's so cheap I'd be a fool not to miss it," she said. "People shouldn't live on top of one another, after all." We were in the fruit store, with the cracked ladders and the copies of *Valmouth*. At the end of the year, books smell damp, fruit smells cheap and out of place; whitewash rubs off the wall at a touch, leaving the whorls of your fingerprints clearly outlined. "We can meet here again, just the way we did! Do you think anyone would buy this?" It was a book-club edition of Peter Fleming, with all the photos torn out. I shrugged and dropped it on to the floor. "And what if we met in a cafe again, by accident? Wouldn't that be strange?" About that time I began to have a dream of an endless conversation between two women:

"I think it's just as well not to be."

"It's just as well."

"I'm over it now you know."

"You're accepting more."

"Yes. Yes. I'm accepting more now."

"I just don't think I could fit into that. It would drive me mad."

"I mean I do so much."

"Of course you do. Of course you do."

"I get so upset."

I often dreamed of Nina too, even after I went to live in Manchester. "Boots off!" she would exclaim, turning her wizened little face up towards the ceiling. "Boots off!"

The first thing I heard Bob Almanac's wife say was,

"What can you do in a town where they pronounce quiche 'keech'?"

91

She was a short, squarish woman, originally from Nottingham-shire, with black hair which she wore in a rough cap. Streaks of grey in it gave her a look of the intelligence and maturity she had submerged in her practical, patient manner; they combined with the lines round her mouth and the hollows at her temples to make you think when you were introduced to her that she was tired. Later you saw that she was holding back some permanent fear or irritation: she imagined she was ill, perhaps, or that she had particularly bad luck.

She worked in the health food shop.

"None of you are getting enough kelp for what you do, of course," I remember her telling me. She glanced at me briefly and cynically, as if she could get from my clothes or the way I stood confirmation of something she already knew. "Those bloody depressions just keep coming up, don't they? One after the other, like clockwork. Just like clockwork. I could graph them out for you on a bit of paper."

And when I could think of nothing to say to this diagnosis:

"Talk to the wall, talk to the wall. Oh well, you'll learn."

I asked Bob if she used her own products.

"Oh yes," said Bob. They both did in fact. They found them very useful. "You've to be sensible about it," he warned me, "and not just to chuck things down you. A lot of people think, for instance, that just because bee-pollen's helped them, zinc will too." He laughed. "Anne's the expert, and I leave it to her."

When he talked about her to us, it was with a kind of wondering admiration. She fasted, he told us, often for four or five days at a time, taking only water and vitamins. While it was apparent that this rather unnerved him, he tried to pass on to us his faith in her judgement. "She'll occasionally get a bit of a headache on the third day, but it's nothing to worry about. All the toxins are coming out by then, you see: the body's beginning to eat itself." He offered us this achievement modestly, on her behalf. We had a picture of her in control of a dangerous equilibrium, like some trapeze artist of the body chemistry. Would she fall? It was possible *to* fall, Bob's manner admitted. But it was the least important part of his job as ringmaster to work us up over that.

After I got to know her I sometimes went into the shop to buy things she or Bob had recommended — magnesium, high-dose capsules of vitamin B, mineral complexes and herbal dietary supplements which would for a week or two dispel my vague lassitudes or make me seem to climb a little better before they lost their effect. It was always empty, and for most of the day she seemed to sit twisted round on a high stool behind the counter, staring out of the window at the zebra crossing or over at the bleak apron of the Civic Centre opposite, where rain shone on the hexagonal paving slabs and the wind ruffled stealthily the shallow puddles, and where at dinner time she might see Gaz lurching along in his clogs eating a pork pie. It gave her a melancholy but intense pleasure to think about what other people ate.

"The things they stuff themselves with," she would say absently as she served you. She had a way of remaining still for a long period after you had given her the money, then laughing shortly and throwing it into the drawer of the wooden till as if it was distasteful to her. Her wrists were thin, the tendons very prominent on the backs of her hands. "The stuff they eat!"

The shop did best at the end of a damp winter, especially towards the end of March. In summer, stock replacement was low. She sold out of the popular lines, and the colourful little packets and plastic tubs that remained seemed to gather dust from the sunlight. When her employers promoted her to manageress and suddenly moved the business into Sawter's Yard, well back from the main street and up a cool alley with ferns growing out of the walls, you could see it was much reduced. They ran it down until it stocked only the hops and equipment for making your own beer; soon after that they closed it altogether. Anne Almanac seemed to close with it, and vanish.

I heard from Normal, who loved a gossip, that she was in London; from someone else that she had gone home to Retford or Worksop or wherever it was that her family still lived. A month or two later she was back. Bob never mentioned that she had been away.

"She's got him well under her thumb," was Normal's opinion. "Well under it."

But I see her like this: in Huddersfield, wondering if she can endure another year of sitting in Marie's restaurant drinking coffee. At the Sainsbury's checkout she hears a woman say, "Alec, get your foot off the biscuits. I shan't tell you again. If you don't get your foot

93

off the biscuits, Alec, I shall knock it straight on the floor." Spring at last, and there is a strong smell of burning plastic along the ring road. The sun moves across the patterned bricks outside the bus station. The buses are parked obliquely while they wait: she gets on to one to take the shopping home, and from the top deck sees across to the next, where a girl is blowing her nose. I think now that she was down to the bone with ambition. Bob perhaps recognised something like that.

"I don't smoke, myself," he would say. "She was sick in the morning sometimes until I gave up smoking. We guessed it was the smell of the ashtrays first thing."

Shortly after they came over from Manchester Normal and his wife moved into one of the new estates which were being built high up on a narrow remnant of moorland between the pipeworks and the M62. It had displaced one or two run-down farms and cottages and a lot of stone walls, and was designed in a crescent shape facing south west. It seemed to have more service roads than an ordinary topology would allow for, going out like spoke after spoke through bleak muddy expanses of new grass. They lived in one of hundreds of small houses with underfloor electric heating and thin interior walls, pebbledashed on the outside, with a yellow front door and varnished wooden panels under each ground floor window. The gales and rain of their first winter there, squirting in parallel to the motorway across Rishworth Moor, fetched the pebbledash off and cracked the paint, while the varnish simply wore away, leaving the wood beneath whitish grey, like the planks of some small boat abandoned on a beach.

Neither of them had owned a house before. Soon after they moved, Normal slipped off a bedside chair and put his foot through the top of the new dressing table.

"I was really gripped. Scent was flying everywhere. I couldn't get my leg out."

He had been trying to hang above the bed a panoramic view of the Aiguilles; later the same day someone saw him in Huddersfield with a piece of chipboard under his arm. He was like a man in a foreign country. You found him in the afternoon in a stone-cold box room levering open a stiff window with a screwdriver. He worked for two days on a project then started something else. Before she would let him leave his job his wife had made him agree to take responsibility for the housework. After that the landing always smelled of unwashed clothes, stuffed into the blue plastic launderette bag under the bathroom sink, and a cold draught blew across the kitchen from the irregular hole he had chiselled in the wall one Saturday for the waste pipe of the plumbed-in Hotpoint.

His wife never knew what to expect when she got home from work. One Wednesday it had been a blowlamp, of all things, going full bore on the bathroom shelf. "No Norman, of course. No Norman anywhere. *He'd* dropped everything to go and fetch some friend of his whose car had broken down in Stoney Middleton." She had looked everywhere, but there was no Norman. "Only this propane blowlamp roaring away not two inches from the plastic tiles. Never mind some climber's car! What about my house?"

Normal grinned slyly across the kitchen table.

"You know you love me. Any more chips? Oh go on: don't be tight!"

This seemed to please her.

"What am I going to do with him?" she would appeal to you. "Norman! Don't eat like that!"

She washed her hands of him: "What would *you* suggest?"

(Going out late from the house one night in January, Mick from the pipeworks answered in a low distinct voice, "Kick the fucker's arse and make him grow up." His breath steamed in the bitter air as he fastened his coat collar and looked along the street. She was standing behind him on the doorstep, but she said nothing and I don't think he knew.)

She had made some effort to decorate the place nicely. In the sitting room they had heavyweight beige wallpaper featuring in relief a venous network, as if someone had stuck the bleached skeletons of leaves on it with great care while it was still wet. Looking closer you saw it was a motif of elm trees, half-abstract, transformed. Against this, on glass shelves and small stacking tables, was displayed her collection of artificial flowers — morning glory a filmy transparent blue, paper sweet peas, orange lilies which

95

looked almost real. She hadn't been collecting them for long but already she had examples from all over the world: some of them were quite valuable and old. At mid-day in the empty room the light illuminated their delicate shabby petals. There was sometimes even a faint scent.

"I know I'm wrong," Normal's wife would say, "but I always associate that with my pansy."

And she would take it down to show you, a crushed, dusty little thing made in the Twenties out of black velvet, the centrepiece of the collection. "Isn't she beautiful? So much nicer than the modern plastic ones! She purrs if you stroke her. Can't you imagine her, pinned on a green tulle dress smelling of California Poppy? Oh, I could never call her 'it'. She's a real personality to me."

The trouble was now that Norman never bought anything but vases. Christmas, birthdays, anniversaries, it was always a vase!

Until the age of seventeen she had been a drum majorette. Among the flowers was a framed photograph of her in the sexless gold-frogged uniform jacket and short pleated white skirt: an unattractive child, named Margaret after the princess, with a wide mouth eager to please and a head of tight American curls. She was even taller now; her cheeks had fattened out. She came from one of the villages south east of Huddersfield along the Wakefield Road. Her father still lived there. It was a dull place, not even picturesque, the houses up close to the road, with aprons of mud splashed up by the heavy traffic, overshadowed by a television transmitter and an unimaginative Victorian folly she called "my castle". She seemed to miss it, and once said to me:

"We're very much on the bleak side of town here."

It was the middle of the afternoon by then. I had found her on her own in the house, her face puffy, as if her eyes and nose had been running. A faint yeasty smell seemed to cling to her faded pink cotton housecoat, and to the wallpaper in the lounge, like the smell of herbal medicines. I thought perhaps she had been taking something for a cold. When I asked if Normal was in she sat down on the maroon imitation-leather sofa and looked away from me. Her feet were bare. It was hot. Behind her on their glass shelves the artificial flowers looked dry and colourless.

"It's just that he was supposed to be collecting me this morning."

I put my bag down in the middle of the carpet, in a bar of light. Once you have decided to go climbing the whole sense of the day, its whole meaning, lies in that. You have dedicated it. It is no longer any use for anything else. At Beeston Tor, at Cratcliffe or Ravensdale, the hard climbs will draw you on after them, into the sunshine out of the wells of shadow. Do anything else and you will still be there. Do anything else and you are only storing up a kind of boneless fatigue for yourself, because it demands as much energy to imagine climbs, to pre-empt them, as it does to climb them. I had been awake early and now I was half asleep. I laughed, and said to Normal's wife to prompt her,

"I thought he might have forgotten me. He's been a bit vague lately!"

Eventually, as if it was an effort, she said:

"You call that 'a bit vague' do you?" And added after some thought: "You climbers?"

The housecoat, I saw, had a design of stylised blue flowers joined by strands of yellow creeper and clusters of washy indigo leaves behind which in a much paler pink, so that they looked ghostly and very far away, were the trees and bridges, the stone pagodas and campaniles of some Chinese Gothic Italianate park. It was too short. She pulled it round her suddenly and stood up. "Do you want some tea?" she said, going over to the kitchen door. "I won't offer you any home-brewed beer, even though we've got forty pints of it on the floor —" She wrenched the door open and the smell I had thought was cold-cure poured in, washing over us like the thick half-fermented reek that fills the car when you drive past a city brewery in the morning.

Before they moved from Manchester she had insisted on fitted kitchen units — remembering how in her childhood someone had repeated that the kitchen was the heart of the house, "the pivot of the household", and getting in a firm from Leeds to measure them up — with melamine fascias meant to represent polished wood, aluminium strips along the recessed handles of the drawers, surfaces that could be cleaned at a wipe. Normal had pulled one of the higher ones off the wall. A plastic barrel had come down with it, spattering sour grey pulp down the wall, along with half a dozen cider bottles which now lay broken on the lino among the detached shelves and other odds and ends — some funnels of different sizes, a length of clear tubing, sodden cardboard packets. When I tried to imagine how he had done it I was surprised to feel a sudden tired contempt for him. The stink was enough to make you sick.

"There!" said his wife. "You see?"

Her desperate theatrical gesture with the door had only caused the housecoat to ride up awkwardly over her naked buttocks, so that I could see the fold of flesh beneath them, and beneath that the dull blue veins on the back of her thighs, the angry red lines where she had sat across one of the seams of the sofa. "It doesn't even smell of beer!" In her misery her face was drawn back into a shiny grin which made her look even more like the counterfeit of the red-cheeked majorette in the photograph. (If you went there in the evening she would tell you towards the end of the meal, "My father keeps all those uniforms. Every time I grew out of one he put it away in tissue paper! Isn't that sweet?")

"If you want to know," she said, "this is what happens when you ask to borrow your own car. I said he could have it back this afternoon, but oh no: that wasn't good enough for Norman." She rubbed her eyes and laughed.

"You climbers have got a lot to learn about him."

She saw me looking at her buttocks.

"Oh *Christ*," she said. She ran out of the room and I heard her going up the stairs. A door slammed.

I couldn't find a mop or a bucket in the kitchen; perhaps I was looking in the wrong place. At the back of the house they had a twenty-five yard strip of garden divided along part of its length by the washing line. The door to it was open so I gave up and went out there with some idea of waiting for Normal.

In his first enthusiasm he had dug it over, put up white board fencing, and started a rock garden in which it was his intention to have a rock from every major crag in Britain. He had a vision of great angular pieces of slate like gravestones, looming up at him out of the wet mist the way they had done *in situ*; lumps and nodules of that metamorphic, bubbly stuff from the sea cliffs at Gogarth, birdlimed or smelling of salt; a garden like a limestone scree which would break out at the right time of year, shady and steep, with ramsons or herb robert or shepherd's purse. "But the biggest bit, right in the middle, will be from Cloggy. Think of it," he would urge us: "A bit of Cloggy in your own back garden!" He had imagined it would put the crag out there for him, leaning up that ferocious golden colour it often has in the morning light. Perhaps it would have done. He sometimes trampled about out there at weekends even now, wearing a pair of Hanwag big-wall boots which rapidly picked up the thick gluey soil. But gaps had appeared in the fence — though he had patched them with scraps of corrugated plastic the black alsatian dog from the house next door still pushed its way through after closing time every night to eat Kentucky Fried Chicken bones on the lawn — and on wet days the concrete path ran out under the washing line like a duckboard on a building site.

It was tranquil in its way. Earlier in the year there had been some great blowsy poppies patched and rimmed with grey as if their lipstick had come off; irises which when their flowers collapsed looked like shreds of coloured Kleenex hanging on a stick. Now insects went busily through the long grass which, heat-browned, had choked the borders. All the gardens were dry that year. The use of hosepipes had been banned. Standpipes, we had heard, were in operation further south.

I sat for half an hour in the sunshine and the dusty smell of chamomile and seeding docks. Two or three gardens along, someone was cutting wood: the saw made its repeated gasping sound against the faint shouts of children playing somewhere over on the edge of the estate. Each gasp rose in tone until the cut wood thudded down on to concrete. This sequence was repeated four or five times, like a woman producing orgasm after orgasm in the sunny back garden, and the smell of creosote came up like the smell of an unguarded physical commitment to the moment. The gasps of the saw, the distant cries of the children, the hot sunshine, combined to produce in me both languor and excitement, each somehow amplifying the other.

Some of the stuff Normal had collected was already embedded in the baked earth as if it had always been there. It had come from the easily-accessible cliffs of the Pennines. Prising one lump out with another I found he had pencilled on them dates and places; but these inscriptions were too blurred or faded to read. A flake of fine-grained sandstone came to light. It was about three feet square, and across it someone — not Normal — had scratched, "Crux hold of Orange Squash, Wilton Three"; and then, with an arrow, the instruction: "Undercling here". I wondered who had been under-clinging it when it came off. As I dropped it back into the pile I heard Normal's wife flush the lavatory; saw out of the corner of my eye a movement behind the net in the window of an upper room.

It was when she came down and saw me looking across the remaining corridor of moorland towards the pipeworks that she said, "We're very much on the bleak side here. When you're not so busy climbing you'll have to come and see how lovely the real Yorkshire can be." She laughed and turned a stone with her foot. She had put on a skirt and a blouse, to which she had pinned the black velvet pansy. "I see you've found the quarry. I call it his quarry."

Attracted perhaps by the smell from the kitchen, an insect buzzed heavily past like someone shouldering his way into a shop; in the next house they switched a radio on, then after some argument off again.

"Your hair's very nice that way," Normal's wife said. "Have you just had it cut?"

I stared at her.

While I still lived with Pauline we went to a "psychic" who gave demonstrations on most weekdays in the North London area. He appealed mainly to women who found they had nothing to do in that part of the afternoon which sags out — especially in winter — between the hairdresser and the children's tea, and he preferred to work in clean but draughty modern halls, panelled with light wood and smelling of polish, used in the evenings for other functions: lectures, Bunuel films, political meetings. There would be a shrouded projector at the back, thick blue velvet curtains, a lectern pushed to the side of the platform.

Sleet touched the tall windows the first time we went. That was in Golders Green, and darkness was already drawing round some shrubs and a bench in the gardens outside. It was odd to sit there at three o'clock in the afternoon among all those women. It had a kind of intimacy.

"Now give him the benefit of the doubt," Pauline had warned me on the tube from Camden. "Or you can just stay outside. It's only an hour."

He was a man of about fifty-five or sixty, tallish, who wore an old-fashioned tweed jacket and whose resonant but haggard professional voice sometimes took on a nicely-judged edge of irritability. He had a practical face: but it was so white and bony you thought immediately of a terminal disease, and of all his practicality committed there, to the control of his own panic. It was his own panic, I suppose, that enabled him to recognise theirs.

"I think we could have the curtains closed," he said.

His method was to work his way along the rows saying to one woman, "You have what I call the artistic temperament," and to another, "You have just returned from that so-difficult trip abroad you feared." He stood awkwardly in the middle of the platform and picked them out by pointing to them, two or three from each row. "Well, there was nothing to be frightened of, was there?" Clearly he was guessing these things from an item of dress or a sun tan; neither did he hide the fact that many of the women were already regulars of his, with habits and circumstances known to him. "Did he buy you that ring in the end dear? And was it *that* ring?"

Yet they sat so patiently, relaxed by the distant hum of traffic making its way down endlessly into the city, nodding and laughing and exclaiming to encourage him. If they couldn't immediately relate to their own lives the things he said, they signalled by willing frowns that they were prepared to puzzle over it. It was after all an insight and they were not going to waste it. It seemed quite sufficient to them.

"You're a woman of the world dear and you know how to help him. I can say that to you I think, can't I, without giving offence?"

He could.

As his hour wore on he sometimes prompted them openly. "I see a lady. An old lady. Yes, I see an old lady and she. Yes, she isn't very well. An old lady in a room. In a room upstairs." Used up in his own struggle to keep from evaporating away, he looked along the rows of seats for help. "Now does anybody here know an old lady like that? I do sense her very strongly, very close. She's very close to us now. Does anybody *remember* an old lady like that? Yes dear? Does that mean something to you, dear? Does it? She's in a red dressing gown and she's reading a book. I can tell you that if it helps. Is it a Bible dear? Does that mean anything to you?"

By now it did. Someone had recognised this spectre as her grandmother, seen once in childhood, after that never again.

"Well she thinks it's time to sell that thing you were talking about, dear," he said. And then, producing their previous exchange, at Belsize Park a week before, as if it was in itself a psychic sleight of hand: "You remember we talked about it last time?"

"Oh yes," she whispered, delighted.

The women near enough to hear her nodded at one another significantly, and also with a sort of angry commonsensical triumph. This was the advice they would have given, all along.

Whenever he felt their attention begin to wander he jerked his head up as if he could hear a voice and said impatiently: "It's no good. I can't tell you what you want if you don't speak clearly." The effort to hear was costly, and made him seem even more ill. It gave his face the inanimate look of a mask, or a painted balloon on a piece of string which someone had tugged sharply towards one of the upper corners of the room and then released. He asked the women puzzledly, "Is there anyone here called Erica or Eileen?" They stared at one another. This time, though they were sympathetic, they were unable to help. One of them had a daughter whose name was Eveline. But the message, elusive, garbled, fragmentary, sporadic as a twitch, didn't seem to be for her.

"Nina's name was going to be 'Ellen'," Pauline said to me later. "That's the funny thing. I was going to call her 'Ellen', but then we thought of Nina."

I was angry with her.

I remembered her boasting to the American boy Martin (*specialité de maison* of another part of her life): "I left the poor man sitting on the running board with his head in his hands. I'd got the Morris off him for twenty pounds less than he wanted!"

But when I reminded her of this she only shrugged. She was watching the Sony with the sound turned down. She started to comb her hair then stopped. "He does better than you ever did at reading minds," she said quietly. On the television a car turned out of some factory gates, slowed down and then raced away suddenly.

I couldn't understand her. It seemed to me then that she had abandoned the protection of an innate, almost provincial shrewdness for the flimsiest and most obviously flawed of reassurances. But I kept going to the demonstrations. One week I was convinced the psychic's pallor was real, the next that he had himself made up before the women arrived — that even his illness was an act, the pretence of being closer to the dead than we were. Pauline was nervous and eager by turns. His presence, anyway, seemed to relax her. She sat hunched forward in the front row with her chin on her hand, and when he came on to the platform he advised her that nothing could be more trouble than your teeth.

"There are other aches though, dear, aren't there?"

He asked her if she had a cat.

If you untie an old knot, Bob Almanac showed me, the original colours of the rope shine out again from a nest of convolutions — pink, yellow, green, orange, much as they were in a quiet shop on a wet afternoon in winter.

"You release the light that was caught up in the knot," he said. "I think of it as releasing the light."

He smiled shyly.

"I thought you'd like that."

Out running in the early morning to avoid the heat, I found three pairs of women's shoes someone had thrown into a ditch at the top of Acres Lane where it bent right to join the Manchester Road. Delicate and open-toed, with very high heels that gave them a radical, racy profile, they were all size four: one pair in black suede, an evening shoe with a brown fur piece at the toe; one in transparent plastic bound at the edges with metallic blue leather; and a pair of light tan leather sandals with a criss-cross arrangement of straps for the upper part of the foot. Inside them in gold lettering was the brand name "Marquise". It was a little worn and faded, but otherwise they seemed well-kept. They were still there when I went back the next day, but by the one after they had gone. I couldn't imagine who would have thrown them there; or, equally, who would pick them up from a dry ditch full of farmer's rubbish at the edge of the moor.

June had emptied itself ungrudgingly. July was following it. Embarrassed by Normal's evasiveness, afraid that in some sense the summer was slipping away from me, I telephoned him.

He seemed cheerful. That morning, he told me, he had taken the front brake shoes off his car. Now it turned out he had bought the wrong size replacements. "Otherwise I'd have called for you, youth. I want to go and have a look at this so-called 'crag of the future' they've found near Buxton." He didn't mention his wife.

"Look, Normal, I think I'll go out with Sankey this weekend."

After a pause he said, "Suit yourself."

PART THREE

SUMMER

10 · ESCAPEES

The world receives you and recedes from you in the same moment. "So much depends on perspective, doesn't it?" Pauline used to say. That was some time before I started climbing. She meant, perhaps, that the moment you step into a landscape it becomes another one.

On Sunday mornings the Railway Cafe at Grindleford is full of school teachers, up from the Midlands by Ford Fiesta to do climbs in the Hard Very Severe and low Extreme grades. They squeeze between the tables in the hot steamy air, shouting and talking and clattering their plates. The men, in their middle thirties, with longish hair and aggressive but neat beards, often teach maths or geography; some of them can play the guitar. They make thoughtful, steady climbers. Though they lack the imagination, the edge of nervous excitement, to be outstanding, they form the backbone of the sport. They occupy its middle ground. They decide its shape. If they have a fault it's that they are too minutely concerned to use in the same way the same holds everyone else has used.

"You won't need chalk for that, Simon," they call to one another peremptorily.

(The local daredevils look down guiltily at their hands then mimic, "'If you haven't done the mantelshelf, Simon, you haven't done the route.'")

They were out at Burbage yesterday, climbing until late: they're really quite pleased to have led Long Tall Sally at last, a bit of a squib but a real calf-wrecker if you hang about on it too long. Today they are going to try something a bit bigger, Welcome To Hard

Times at Staden Quarry. "Might as well have a go as not!" Last week, although they know it's pretty hard to believe, they were rained off Tremadoc; next week they thought they might go and have a look at Subluminal Cliff, Swanage, start getting some ticks in *Rock Climbing in Britain*!

"How much salt are you going to put on that egg?"

"Yes, come on now," his wife reminds him, "leave some for the rest of us, Tom! *Tom*!"

Laughter.

"What delights have you got in store for us today then, Tom?"

"How do I know?" grunts Tom. "Until I get a sight of the guide book?"

They always begin here, or at Eric's cafe, Stoney Middleton or Pete's Eats in Llanberis or Eric Jones's on the A498, places confusingly similar, with an ideal smell of exhaust smoke and deep-fat frying, where there are faded climbing photos curling from the walls and a new-routes book on the counter by the sugar bowl and you can get a pint mug of tea to wash down your full-set breakfast of sausage, bacon, eggs, baked beans, tomatoes, fried bread, bread and butter. In the evenings you will find them drinking in the Radjel, the Moon, or the Pen y Gwrd.

It's a bit of tradition with them. The women, older than you think in their stretch nylon Tracksters and striped singlets, subscribe to it especially. Most of them climb a little. More than anything, they have adapted nicely to the demands of a sham-peripatetic existence. They are doing a sort of part-time degree in English at Solihull. As well as climbing they are interested in printing for the community.

Today, though, one of them looks ahead suddenly as the food is passed across the tables. She's inexplicably bored and lonely. Yesterday she sprawled all afternoon among the warm boulders in the sun. She didn't feel like climbing, although Derek had found a really good Hard Severe for her at Burbage, with an apt name, Amazon Crack. That morning he had met, quite by accident, a friend of his from Sheffield University years ago. Of all things he turned out to be in computers! They decided to go on to Gardom's Edge. She laughed at their private jokes, watched them top-rope Moyer's Buttress — "I'm running out of strength!" "Go on Derek, *push*!" — and read Herman Hesse (*The Glass Bead Game*). Then she fell asleep, half-listening to the insects in the bracken. When she woke it was suddenly, with the warm dusty smell of the rock in her nostrils, surprised that time had passed, desperate for a pee but not daring to go with so many tourists about.

She noticed the most beautiful little beetle, climbing up the back of one of Derek's boots, a perfect shiny metallic green colour, like anodised aluminium. After a moment or two it dropped off and waved its legs in the air.

"Derek, it's eight o'clock!"

Now she watches him pushing the fried bread fussily across his plate with a fork; and he says to his friend:

"Remember the Doncaster half-marathon, Simon?"

"1981! I was about a second behind Duckham and you were about eight seconds adrift. Oh, seven was it, I remembered it as nearer eight."

They laugh in unison and look at her.

"Anyway, that was when he lost his shoe!"

If she slides her chair back she can see out of the window: a part of the railway bridge, trees, a car parked with its nearside wheels in a long puddle. Some hikers come past with their trousers tucked into their socks. The cafe dog, a big alsatian, looks up. More climbers are eating out there, grouped round the weathered grey tables in the ten o'clock sun. A boy nineteen or twenty years old stands out from the rest. His hair is dyed dark red and worn in plaited rats'-tails down his back; his arms are thin and white, and will show no muscle until he locks them off later in the day soloing Quietus Stanage, which he nearly falls off; he has on elegant dirty fatigue trousers and a T-shirt with the sleeves torn out. He is teasing the dog with the remains of his breakfast.

"Look at this!" he shouts. And then to the dog, "Hey!", snatching the food away at the last moment, offering it and snatching it away until with a look of understanding the dog loses interest and moves away.

He gets up and begins to walk about, hissing and whistling, scuffing his feet, sits down again. "Where we going? Where we going today?" he asks his friends. "Are we going now? Let's go!"

then, sensing perhaps that she is watching him, reaches out quickly and catches a wasp with his fingers. "Hey! Look! I got it!" He blinks ecstatically; she turns away with a sudden feeling of amusement, only to hear,

"Are you sure it was seven? I definitely had the impression it was eight."

"Have some Rice Krispies on your sugar!"

Someone farts.

"Oh God, that's just antisocial, Tom!"

"Yes, if you're going to do that, turn your bum in another direction!"

"Ha."

"A ha ha ha."

You meet her two years later at Burbage in June, and find her climbing with the boy. She leads a Difficult while he sits boredly underneath holding the rope, occasionally looking up her shorts. Woven into her bootlaces are little hearts; into his, stars. "Because," she tells you seriously, "he's a star." And although you've never heard of him, he does climb well.

All through August the teachers are in France or Italy, climbing at Buoux or in the Alps or Verdon. They always try to get away somewhere different in the summer. In the packed lay-bys beneath the popular crags, their Fords and Renaults and Fiats are immediately replaced by the "Sunshine Coaches" of the Variety Club of Great Britain. You find these white minibuses full of city children parked half-on and half-off the grass verges of narrow roads all over the Peak District: Stanage, Bamford, Baslow; all along the A57 "Snake"; as far north as Pule Hill and as far south as Dovedale. From them, harassed men and women dressed in the fashion of Fifties hairdressers lead walks round the local beauty spots.

The children always seem emotionally as well as socially deprived: big vague boys with a hit-and-miss way of walking, as though they needed all their attention to oversee their legs; enormously fat girls in early adolescence, panting and sweating and suffering with their huge breasts in the heat, who wear a red skirt and a yellow cardigan; a small boy dawdling at the back, surreptitiously pulling at the seam of his trousers as if it is chafing his bottom.

"Come down off there Joan. I don't think that's very clever."

They wind away up through the bracken, yelling and getting smaller. At the end of the afternoon there are inevitably one or two missing. The minibus driver waits twenty minutes; he shrugs and drives off slowly towards the Ladybower Dam, Glossop, and from there to Salford.

Over the following months, the escaped children learn to live by begging from the long lines of ramblers which lie permanently across the moors on Sundays like florists' ribbon. They begin by asking for money — ten pence, twenty pence — "to get home", although they are already forgetting where their homes were. They end up fighting over the discarded sandwich wrappers which float in the updraughts on the edge of the Kinder Escarpment. The fat girls soon become lean and muscular, and move with a fiercely agile gait between the piled boulders; while at the slightest sound the awkward boys make off farting, with a sudden breathtaking burst of energy, to some cave beneath the summit of the rocks. In the mornings they find themselves looking at a flower or a cloud; they see themselves by accident in the "Mermaid's Pool" and pause for a second, puzzled. Their clothes have long ago deteriorated and fallen away.

In winter, the death toll is savage. Those that survive learn to cope with the continual wind and rain, the bitter nights and damp blowing snow of the watershed, by forming loose unhierarchical groups. They know the insulating power of dead bracken. When there are no more ramblers, the girls might run down a sheep: three or four flickers of naked white speed against the rain and the endless black peat rollers: a fire in the night. A girl on her own will not light a fire, but get into the warm carcass and curl up instead, to conserve heat.

Air Force Cadets, Boy Scouts and teenage charity walkers, lost on the long hikes which would have initiated them as useful members of society at large, are adopted eventually by this regime of wild children. Who hasn't caught a glimpse of them at one time or another on the moor, pale and naked, running with that super-naturally confident gait between the tracts of bog cotton?

Living along the gritstone edges, and soon forgetting any other existence, they become like lemurs, like ghosts. In some way the rocks and the climbs come to belong to them. They allow us to see only dream rocks, dream climbs. This is what Sheffield climbers believe. Silent Spring, The Knock, Above & Beyond the Kinaesthetic Barrier with its eerie tangle of 6b moves: all only shadows. To have had first ascents at all, they must already have been climbed by the escaped girls. In this way, it is maintained in Sheffield, areas of rock hitherto unclimbable are "released" to the hardest and most visionary technicians, who, to encourage the children, leave them gifts of food, cigarettes and equipment.

When Bob Almanac told me about the Variety Club children, I felt a sudden unbearable compassion for their adolescence as it passed: the mornings by the pool, the light blonde down on the arms, the eyes narrowing bemusedly in the bright sunlight, the dumb awareness of the sexual organs. I asked him: "What happens when they grow up?"

"They become people like you and me," said Bob. "They reinstate themselves slowly into human affairs." He winked. "After a few years no one knows."

11 · THE NUMBERS

There are climbs whose secret is a succession of moves — like the enchained steps of a ballet — sometimes so intricate that the likelihood of your working it out by trial and error is directly dependent on the number of falls you are prepared to take from it. Yorkshire climbers often call this sequence 'the numbers'. Tourists watch them in the evening at the bottom of the great central wall of

Malham Cove, pivoting suddenly away from the little holds as if they have grown shy, one arm thrown backwards, an expression halfway between surprise and excitement on their faces. They seem to hang there forever in the soft warm quiet air, like photographs of themselves, before they begin to fall. Learning the numbers: to what end, perhaps, they are less and less sure.

12 · SANKEY AND HIS SISTER

"What are you doing with all that money you're making, Sankey?"

For a moment Sankey, leaning forward over the pub table, had a look on his face as delicate as a girl's. Then he said,

"Buggered if I know lad. Tax man gets most of it I suppose."

No-one expected more. Some kind of evasion, a covering of his tracks, had always been normal to him. He had once told me, for instance, that his teeth were false. "They're more trouble than they're worth, kid, your own teeth," he said. One night after a dream in which he was looking down a deep stinking hole, he'd woken up to find an awful smell in his cottage. "I thought, 'That'll be why I had the dream, then.' I got up and looked round for a bit, but I couldn't find anything. I even went downstairs and had a look in the sink. Then I realised it was my own mouth. Nearly puked. Went and had them out the next day."

But later when I referred to this story he insisted,

"I don't know where you got that idea from, kid. I've always taken good care of my teeth." He seemed huffy.

How much of himself did he conceal behind manoeuvres like this? I don't remember wondering. It was a long time before I learned what he did for a living. Bob Almanac told you one thing, Normal another, and soon I saw that neither of them actually knew. Some climbers thought he was in computing, others that he worked for a firm of electrical engineers on Chapel Hill in Huddersfield. From the hints he dropped it could have been either. Whatever it was, he was notoriously mean with what he earned at it.

Every Christmas Day he went to a sister of his. She gave him a woollen hat to climb in. What he gave her in return I can't imagine. When I knew him, he was still wearing the first one she had ever given him. The rest were in a drawer, perhaps a dozen woollen bobble hats, a bit stretchy on the head, in white and one other colour: hats going back for years, enough hats for the rest of his life.

"They're good hats these, kid," he would say. "Really last well."

There was a kind of self-expatriation in the way he lived by himself in the cottage under the edge of the moor. It had concentrated his forces so that he hadn't much need for anyone. In the end, though, this tended to alienate the other climbers. You saw he was interested in them only because their share of the petrol money would lower the cost of a day out in a car whose fuel-economy was already a legend. His evasiveness galled people; his self-sufficiency was revealed as a statement of policy rather than a way of life. I remember him sitting on a bench outside the cafe at Stoney Middleton because he felt sick. That was before I climbed regularly with him. It was a freezing cold day in April and he thought he had some virus that was going round at work. "I can't seem to get warm somehow," he complained. He had been complaining all morning. I made him have a cup of tea and in the end persuaded him to come inside and drink it. Out of the window we could see snow falling through the sunlight.

"It'll be like this for a month now," Sankey told me. "The weather." I asked him if he'd like to give up for the day and go home and he said, "You might as well feel ill out here, kid, as at home on your own." When I repeated this to Bob Almanac later he laughed and suggested,

"Ask yourself who paid for the tea."

I thought this revealed more about him than it did about Sankey.

"Come on, Bob," I said. "Be fair."

Sankey decided he wanted to get out to a place called Whitestone-cliffe, or White Mare Crag, near Sutton Bank in the Hambledon

Hills, one of several shaky teeth in that gum where it curves east above the Yorkshire Plain.

It was a hot day. We were in running shorts, with Sankey's dusty old ropes draped round our necks; I had bought us a lot of soft drinks. "Water's cheaper," Sankey advised me. (He kept his in a dented aluminium bottle which he had used in the Alps to carry cooking fuel and which nobody else would drink out of.)

"I haven't been here for a year or two."

From the scenic car park, with its waste bins full of wine bottles and Peau Douce disposable nappies, he found a sunny little path through some woods, narrowed by colonies of dog rose and bramble, filled with the dozy hum of insects so that it seemed like the path that runs along the bottom of some secluded, overgrown town back garden, then suddenly opening right up on the edge of the escarpment so that you felt as if you were flying. One step sideways and you could have drifted out over Gormire Lake, a Victorian brooch oval and dark in the drenching sunshine, while below you the A170 stretched just like a bored cat before flinging itself up the huge earthwork of the Clevelands.

"They found a woman's body here," Sankey told me seriously. "It were in a dry-cleaning bag." He considered this. "Aye, a plastic dry-cleaner's bag, that were it. She were in her thirties, so they said. Just behind the car park as was."

The cliff is quite a tall one. Steep soil-creep terraces overgrown with willow-herb lead down to its base, where sections have fallen away over the years to produce its substantial roofs and overhangs like a motorway flyover among rumours of corrupt contracting — poor materials, backhanders, bankruptcy. The rock is a kind of crumbling yellow cement stuffed with pebbles, adulterated with sand, propped up here and there by paving slabs of harder stuff bedded so that you can slot them in and out. In some places it has a spurious warm honey colour in the sun; elsewhere it looks like the cheese it is.

"You're usually all right," said Sankey, "if you keep to the cracks. The rock round them seems that bit more reliable."

He claimed he had been on it regularly with two or three Yorkshire teams while it was still an aid-climbing venue, adding quickly that to climb there was more of a Cleveland tradition: "It were lads from Cleveland did most on it. Some of them were free-climbing here even in the Sixties." While I sat there reluctantly uncoiling the rope he pointed out a system of cracks which slipped between the biggest overhangs. "I remember it as quite easy, this one. Technically, I mean. What makes it interesting is it's just that bit loose."

"Wonderful," I said.

"Oh, you'll have no trouble. You're not the sort to go grabbing stuff and swinging about on it. Thing is, it's technically easy but just slightly loose you see, so you've to treat it with a bit of respect." He looked up hopefully. "I'm almost certain it followed these cracks. There might be an aid move or two left on it."

I watched him through the overhangs and out of sight. After that there was only the movement of the rope, the steady patter of small stones and sand like rain on dry leaves in a summer shower. Heat blew back off the rock. Harvest machinery clacked and groaned in the distance; closer to, insects were buzzing and blundering about among the boulders. "How does it look?" I shouted to Sankey. No answer. I could hear his breath going in and out like coal being shovelled; he sounded a long way up. If I sat back and strained my neck I could just see him: the angle of the rock was such that he disappeared again almost immediately. I felt thirsty but I couldn't get the Tizer open without letting go of the rope. In the end I wiped the cold tin over my cheeks and neck instead, and this made me think suddenly of a post office in some village somewhere — Ingleton or Trewellard or Porthmadoc — where in a corner of the small refrigerator among the ice creams there are always a few packs of Birds Eye beefburgers frozen into a lump with a sundae in a plastic tub shaped like a goblet. The colours of the sundae have dulled with frost, and it is hard to eat; they separate the beefburgers for you with a bread knife. "Watch the rope," said Sankey irritably.

The block he was pulling on had begun to tilt. Before he could get his weight off it, it came out. He floated into view fifty or sixty feet above, his runners ripping one by one as his weight came on them — you could see the puffs of dust like little explosions as they smashed the crack apart.

At first his back was towards me, and he was clutching the block: it was squarish, about twenty inches on a side, and he had his arms wrapped tightly round it as if it contained a portable television he had just bought. But then it seemed to detach itself from him, very slowly; while just as slowly he turned over, spreading his arms like a swimmer under water, until I could see the expression on his face. It was neither panicky nor blank, but some indecipherable, almost comical combination of both. Quite suddenly the block accelerated back to the speed of ordinary events, tore through a tree five or ten feet from where I was standing, and was catapulted outwards tumbling over and over through the air.

Surprised by the violence of this I fell down. At the same time the rope ran out through the Sticht plate as if I had caught some enormous fish, and there was Sankey dangling upside down not very far from my head, gaping like a failed Peter Pan, with that passive unreadable expression fading from his eyes.

"Fucking hell," he said. "Ha ha."

The block went on bouncing down the slopes below Whitestone-cliffe. We listened to it for a long time the way people must listen in the aftermath of an explosion, as it rolled and thumped about among the trees, bursting through cool tunnels of foliage and setting up slides of smaller stones, leaving a trail of scarred hawthorn branches and ploughed-up dirt. Eventually it stopped.

"Fucking hell," Sankey repeated. "Eh?"

Bunches of leaves were still drifting down out of the tree.

"Only one of these ropes is holding you," I said. "And I've burnt myself."

Before the belay plate locked, several feet of rope had whipped through my left hand. It hurt, but when I made myself unclench it all I could find was a stiff, melted-looking patch in the middle of the palm, one or two small blisters on the top and second joints of each finger.

"It's not as bad as I thought," I admitted.

Something sly and amused flickered for a moment in the corner of Sankey's eye.

"It never is," he said, "is it? Never as bad as you think."

He turned himself upright on the rope with a quick wriggling motion and swung back on to the route. "I'll get going then," he said. "If you're OK." Immediately he began to climb again as if nothing had happened.

"Christ, Sankey!"

I had no option but to follow. I saw that I would have to move quickly through a region of creaking flakes — they had been pasted on with the cheapest cement — where the climb overhung gently but persistently so that your weight was always on your arms. Holds fell off as soon as I touched them. Every time the rope moved I expected it to fetch more loose stuff out on my head: and I felt dazed, awkward, reluctant to climb, as if this had already happened. "Take in, Sankey. Fucking hell, take in!" A cluster of aid moves turned up at about sixty feet. Just out of reach above a bulge studded with bent, rusty pegs, was a bleached wooden wedge, hammered into the crack some time in the early Sixties. Nobody had done this sort of climbing seriously since then. I got some slings off my harness — they fluttered round me uncontrollably for a moment, blue and fluorescent green, in the hot wind — stood in them and made a wild lunge for the wedge. One of the old pegs broke and I found myself hanging in a tangle of 3,000kg tape, with my left hand trapped behind a snaplink by my own bodyweight and nothing but clear air beneath me all the way down to Gormire Lake, which I could see very small and sharp-cut in the sun like a view in a colour slide. Sand smoked away from the underside of the bulge; bits of rubble fell out of it and went spinning down.

"You bastard," I said.

I fastened everything into the highest peg, jerked into a standing position in the slings, and snatched for the wedge. Once: twice: again. Again. Even when I reached it I found I couldn't release my trapped hand. The whole system had locked into place: it was impossible to lift myself off it, and the strength was going out of my arm. I began to understand the cynicism of Sankey's "You're not the sort to go grabbing stuff and swinging about on it." The climb couldn't be done in any other way. That was its paradox. That was where its value lay.

"Oh *fuck*!" I shouted up at him. "I hate this!"

During the struggle my blisters had burst and some thick dark red blood oozed out of them. It was the only blood we saw in the whole incident, though Sankey had fallen twenty feet or more before the Sticht plate engaged. All his runners had been nuts placed in poor rock, or *in situ* channel pegs rusted to a gesture. He couldn't remember how many of them had failed before something held him. He had a reputation for being cautious but during the time I was with him he repeatedly climbed himself into similar situations. His only fear was that he would take a long fall on the old waistbelt. "I don't know which would be worst, if it broke or if it didn't!"

On the way home from Whitestonecliffe it was hard to talk fast enough. I can't now remember what we said. Our sense of relief ran on into such an incoherent jumble we hardly knew which of us was speaking anyway. "You should have seen your face!" ("I thought I were dead.") "Fucking great branch ripping right off! Five inches thick!" "The runners just popped." ("I thought I'd had it then!") "I knew what you thought, fucking hell I thought you were dead then!" "Fucking hell." And so on until we were laughing and shouting at the tops of our voices at one another while the yellow Reliant wobbled down the A170 at fifty miles an hour. Every so often, as if to emphasise how pleased and excited he was, not just by the narrowness of his escape but by its circumstances too, Sankey gripped the steering wheel harder and, like a racing driver he must have seen in some old film when he was a boy, made a great play of pumping his elbows, rolling his shoulders and squirming about in his seat. He urged the three-wheeler on with his buttocks, and it rocked from one carriageway to the other.

"Fancy an ice cream, kid?"

"Do I!"

In a little shop near York, Sankey put the back of his hand against the caked ice inside the refrigerator then touched it to his face. "And a bag of Alien Spacers, please." Two women in white summer dresses came in and, eyeing his torn vest, pushed past him to the counter. I saw their perfume envelop him. The next morning my fingers were perfectly all right; but my left knee was stiff all day. I couldn't remember banging my knee, but then you never do. When I looked at it there was no bruise.

*

If you mentioned some incident like that to Sankey a week or two later he would look at you vaguely for a moment — as if he couldn't quite place it but felt that would be too abrupt an admission to make — then say, "Oh aye kid, that were a right gripper."

He gave his shy smile, his eyes sliding away from you so that he seemed to be looking at you from the whites.

"It were a gripper right enough."

In fact his memory was good. He had an almost supernatural fund of experience. But climbs and techniques, falls and difficulties, overlapped for him like a pile of colour transparencies, each one lighted so that only a detail stood out, a line of holds leading up to a crack, three fingers locked sideways into a limestone pocket and then shifted suddenly so that he could pull upwards on them, a new way of tying an old knot. A gritstone corner in Yorkshire would suddenly have superimposed on it some of the dynamics of a boulder problem he had done in Joshua Tree in 1972.

"Half the time he doesn't know where he is any more," Normal would complain.

But Sankey knew exactly that: the climb, the moves necessary to complete it or survive it, existed for him solely as an excuse, as a phantom of his own sense of absolute personal orientation. The times I climbed with him his only piece of advice was this:

"You never get away with a fall, kid. It always has some effect on you."

Mick from the pipeworks shrugged this off.

"He'd have more chance if he didn't wear that fucking old waist belt," was all Mick would say. And when I told him, "Sankey didn't seem to be all that certain which route we were on at Whitestonecliffe," he answered, "Oh he knew where he was all right. Only a lunatic would have gone there with him in the first place."

He looked at me in disgust.

"He's trying to strip the last few aid-points off that fucker before the Cleveland lads get it. He wants his name in the magazines."

"You never know what to make of Sankey," I said, "do you?"

"Speak for yourself."

Mick and I didn't have much in common (although once, when

he saw me writing in my notebook, he said almost sympathetically, as if he knew and understood the pressures of obsession, "Do you have to put down everywhere you've bin, then?"), but he had given up his sweeping job in disgust at last, so I could sometimes go climbing with him during the week when Sankey was at work. He did his best with me, but lost his temper easily. We often ended up at Stoney Middleton, where the walls and white ruined-looking pinnacles of the cliff went up ivy-covered over some cottage gardens and an empty garage forecourt.

"It's a great spot," Normal once told me, with uncharacteristic irony.

Limestone dust from the big quarry workings on the other side of the A623 sifted down invisibly all day to be sublimated as a whitish filth on the rose trellises and parked cars. It choked the stream. Further up Middleton Dale, near the Eyam turn, a virus disease had attacked the leaves of the younger trees and turned them black. In late summer the fireweed silk looked like fibreglass waste. Winter revealed poached, aimless-looking tracks beneath the crag, fringed with withered nettles. It was already a popular venue for the Sheffield climbers eager to practise techniques learned in Europe, though they hadn't yet taken to wearing lycra tights and surfing T-shirts. To make them feel at home, heavy vehicles rumbled past twenty yards away, and in the packed black soil you could find broken glass, charred tin cans and hundreds of fragments of pottery.

The first time we went Mick had been laid off with a popped tendon. Because of this he didn't want to do anything hard, he said, so we started at Carl's Wark, two walls varying in height from forty to eighty feet, hinged at a vertical corner and divided up by cracks and bedding planes like the handful of lines on a Constructivist canvas. There is a hole in the ground beneath one of them, out of which a cold wind will issue suddenly on the hottest day. Conversely, in the winter warm air comes out of these cave systems and melts the snow. Groups of local cavers with ten pounds of gelignite in the back of a Bedford van scour the dale for new entrances, prepared to bomb their way in. They are short, with thick beards, and in the Rose and Crown, Eyam, keep themselves to themselves, poring all evening over the crossword puzzle in the *Yorkshire Post*.

Mick had no sooner started up a climb called Carl's Wark Crack when two figures dressed in muddy wet-suits wriggled up into the light from this hole, blinking. It seemed to take them a long time. Black and cumbersome, striped at each seam with bright yellow tape, they looked as juicy as caterpillars. "Then Alex dropped the ammunition box," we heard one of them say as they forced themselves out. "Ah ha ha ha." He didn't sound local. When he raised his arms his rubber elbow patches flapped untidily.

"The stupid divot," his friend said.

"Ah ha ha."

Weaving a little as if dazed they pushed their way through the scaly undergrowth towards the road.

"They must be mad," said Mick with a shiver. He hated to be shut in. "It's dark, it's freezing down there, and it fucking stinks."

He glanced down into the hole, which was directly beneath him, then quickly away.

"They ought to have more sense," he said.

He wasn't doing well. Popular limestone routes take a tremendous polish simply from being touched, like the stones of some shrine. The rock of even a newish climb looks like sweat-stained marble, blackened at crucial points with friction rubber, caked with chalk. Where it would accept them, Mick had worked his slippery hands into the crack. To keep them there he had to change feet constantly, twisting his body one way or the other as balance demanded, gaining an inch or two at a time. This didn't suit his normal style of climbing, in which every move was informed by a barely suppressed fury — a kind of pouncing across the rock from hold to hold.

"Oh fuck I can't remember how to do this," he said.

Every time he had to use his damaged finger he said quietly, "Cunt. You cunt."

Eventually he discovered a shallow pocket for his hands, and by working the toes of his boots into the crack managed to distribute his weight more or less comfortably. This enabled him to admit he couldn't get any further.

"I'm coming down."

As he said this the cavers were making their way back awkwardly through the trees, suits shiny with water. Had they been to wash themselves in the stream? Or simply taken a wrong turning somewhere — one they would never have taken down there in the dark — and fallen in? They stared up at Mick as if they didn't remember him writhing and cursing above them when they emerged from the system, then they began to climb a bit of faded, muddy rope which someone seemed to have dangled for them like an old sash cord down the corner. Their tapes and harnesses were greyish and undependable-looking; they ascended tiredly, with a clanking sound. Their great brown industrial boots scrabbled for a second on the glassy lip of Carl's Wark, then vanished. They pulled the rope up after them.

Mick watched them until they were out of sight. Then he said, "I can't be bothered downclimbing this. Watch the rope," and jumped off.

He was about five feet above his only runner. The impact as he hit it dragged me towards the hole and then over it, so that I had a brief glimpse of narrow contorted slimy walls as polished as the ones above, then hauled me up into the air. On his way down, Mick got my head rammed between his legs. "Christ," he whispered. For a long moment we dangled there, one on each end of the rope, staring into one another's faces, three or four feet above the hole, out of which came a chilly, foul smelling draught — "As if the whole world had farted," Mick explained to someone later. I looked up at the runner, wondering how long it would hold us. Mick shook his head slowly, a curious expression of bleakness and disbelief on his face.

"You incompetent fucker," he said. He laughed. "Let's go and have a snack."

Food obsessed him. As soon as he had finished climbing all he wanted to do was eat; when he wasn't eating it was all he ever talked about. He would describe to us meals he had eaten in canteens, meals he had seen through cafe windows in Leeds in the rain; meals he had always imagined having.

"Fucking hell," he would exclaim suddenly into a silence as Gaz bounced the Vauxhall round the moorland bends of the B6054 (spinning one strand of that tranced, instinctual web we threw over the Peak District in July and August). "Fucking hell! Fish in a tea-cake, wi' salad cream and tomato sauce — grill some fucking Dairylea cheese on it. Fish in a tea-cake!" This was not so much a recipe as a celebration, and reminded him immediately of something else. "Hey! 'Ave you 'ad that stuff you squeeze like toothpaste?" He had eaten a whole tube once, shrimp flavour, in Cornwall after seven pints of Flowers at the Gurnard's Head. "Spewed up all the next day."

Out camping he ate stew and rice pudding from the same plate, and always kept his pans filthy. Every time he got an upset stomach he complained, "I can't understand it, I've never 'ad trouble like this before, I've always et out of dirty pans. That rain must 'ave washed summat down the stream —"

He watched the food like a hawk. He watched you fetch the cardboard box out of the back of the car, he watched you open the tins. He watched the stuff cook, and he watched his own hands as they doled it out — they were like the hands of a priest. He would count the number of chocolate creams in a packet of Fox's Mixed Biscuits. "Keep your eye on Mick," his friends warned, implying perhaps that he got more than his proper share. "You fucking gannets," he accused them. He watched food only because he loved it, and when he wasn't climbing immediately began to put on weight.

Sometimes he would stare into space for a long time and then say confidentially, whether you had asked or not,

"I were trying to remember what I'd 'ad last night."

My knee ached if I walked more than a mile.

"I must have pulled something," I told Sankey, "when we were at Whitestonecliffe."

He looked at me vaguely. "Oh aye, kid?" he said.

In the end I got an appointment with the doctor one Saturday morning.

The wind rolled an empty bottle across the sunny flagstones outside the surgery. Late blossom from a tree I didn't recognise was falling like snow round the girls in their thin white dresses. I could feel Bob Almanac's wife watching me from behind the cash register of the health food shop. She regarded the doctor as a professional equal, but one with only a partial grasp of the more important parts of the trade.

"You'll never learn, you people," I could imagine her saying to me later: "Still, why should I care?"

Inside, I leafed through a copy of *Woman's Own*. While I was waiting for my turn an old man came in, sat down next to a woman further up the queue, and without any preamble said, "I've had this persistent diarrhoea." Perhaps they already knew one another. Perhaps he knew anyway that she would respond: he was one of those Yorkshiremen who have been taken care of for so long by women they still look like children when they are sixty — gazing round from the front seat on the top deck of the bus, bottom lip drooping with excitement, they make a great lip-smacking performance of sucking a cough sweet. They all have very blue eyes.

"Be sensible about it," the doctor said, "and it will go back of its own accord." I had partly displaced the cartilage, he thought. "Only do what you normally would."

I cleared my throat.

"Right," I said.

Did he mean climbing? I wasn't going to ask. I left the surgery with a prescription for ninety tablets of Brufen, one three times a day with or after food. They were pink, but in the bottle they looked orange, and very like Smarties. After I had filled the prescription I went up the steep zigzag streets behind the town and on to the edge of the moor. There were tortoiseshell butterflies opening and closing their wings, like mechanical flowers, on all the thistles in the grass verges.

Sankey had been planning to build an extension to his house.

When I called he was making a trench for the foundations. "It's the right weather for digging," he said, indicating a wheelbarrow full of greyish crumbly soil. In one or two places he had got down to the rock the cottage was built on. After we had talked for a few minutes he said,

"I usually have a brew about quarter past twelve."

I took that to mean he would like to dig until then so I went and sat among the boulders above the house. The wind was cool, the sun warm: the boulders had a bare clean look, sharp-edged and distinct where in the winter they had bulged out softly like a thickening of the mist. To the south, sunshine flared off the windscreen of an infinitely distant car as it dropped through the bends of the A6204. Whatever the doctor had done to it made my knee ache and click. I put my magic boots on and tried a few moves. Sankey had the trench measured out methodically, and I suspected he had set himself goals. I went back a little after the time, to find him solemnly eating bread and cheese and drinking tea.

"Milk, kid?"

When he saw me taking the Brufen he shook his head.

"You want to look after your knees," he said. "I buggered mine ice-climbing." Ice-climbing, he said, was as bad for your knees as football. "You're kicking the crampons in all the time you see, kid," he explained. "It's just kick, kick, kick."

He was thinking, he told me, of changing his car. There were piles of glossy brochures on the sideboard, full of French and Japanese hatchbacks. "I fancy one of these Sumbaroos," he said, showing me a Subaru with four-wheel drive, "except for the servicing." He said 'epsept'. When he was in charge of the map or the guidebook, you never got a clear idea of where you were. Sankey, rendering Bilton as Blighton, would take you up cracks called Pzdn and Trigulph, walls named Quernx. As a boy in the 1950s, I guessed, he had learned from some Yorkshire schoolmistress the need to mumble defensively as he read, eliding the vowels into an approximate buzz.

"Mind you, I've driven the Reliant to the Alps and back."

Unlike Mick, whose flamboyant pounces and sudden balletic shifts of weight sometimes made him look like three frames of a Marvel comic, or Normal, who dragged himself about by his hands, making progressively less and less use of his feet, Sankey climbed with the neat, professionalised moves of a survivor. We spent the afternoon on the boulders, where he set targets and worked as steadily towards them as he had done in his trench. To begin with he seemed old and stiff, groaning as he pulled himself over the top of each problem; later, as he warmed up and began climbing fluently, his youth returned to him, especially about the face and eyes.

After about fifteen minutes he took off his shirt and rolled his trousers up above his knees. The sun made him grin aimlessly. "Warm now," he said, not precisely to me; I felt he would have said it whether I was there or not. "Ha ha." Suddenly he shot backwards off an overhang and rolled over and over in the grass underneath it, propelled not by gravity but by the release of the mechanical energy which had held him in place.

"Dog shit's the worst thing here," he said, getting up.

He thought for a second.

"It's convenient for the house though."

He trained up here in most weathers, he told me, except January and February.

"I hate the first two months of the year," he added, a bit bleakly. "Well, you do, don't you?"

None of the problems were more than thirty feet high, most were between ten and twenty, but to do all of them took him three hours of fairly continuous effort, during which time he climbed perhaps fifteen hundred feet. He kept his eye on me and every so often, when he stopped for a breather, said, "You'd do better if you got your foot higher on that to start with, kid," or: "Most people do that one as a layback." (He referred to 'most people' as a way of gently asserting his experience.) I found that if I had the courage to follow it, his advice was good. But I soon stopped trying to keep up and, muscles already stiffening in the wind, took to wandering about after him watching him climb.

"People bring their dogs all the way up here for a shit," he kept repeating. "That's what I can't see. I can't quite see the logic of that." But he seemed happy enough.

I left him at five o'clock, making himself another brew. He offered me a biscuit before I went outside: he said, "I'll put another hour or so in this evening."

It was hard to guess what Sankey got up to on his own. Apart from climbing guidebooks and magazines stuffed haphazardly into the shelves either side of the fire, his only reading matter was *Samson*, by the Welsh climber Menlove Edwards; and *Treasure Island*, which he had in an illustrated children's edition. "I love the pirates," he would say, "I love the way they talk," and quote:

"'We're that near the gibbet that my neck's stiff with thinking on it'," or, "'If ever a seaman wanted drugs, it's me'." Other than that he had his job; the television, which was hardly ever on; and the yearly visit to his sister, source of a constant if desultory speculation among the other climbers —

Normal would tell you with one breath that Sankey's sister lived in Sheffield; and with the next that it was Derby or perhaps Birmingham, where she was married to a telephone engineer. "One thing's certain," he would say significantly, "she's a lot older than him." Bob Almanac, on the contrary, thought she was a fair bit younger, and that — though nobody had ever met the brother — she was actually Sankey's sister-in-law; they lived locally but were 'close', that is, they kept themselves to themselves. These theories stood out among others as innocent and blurry as the world seen through a frosted glass back door — she was a southerner, she was his cousin, they weren't related at all and she kept a wool-shop in Barnsley. When I thought about it I imagined Sankey's Christmas visit to be much the same as the yearly do at Mick's house, a tall back-to-back in Cooper Lane.

For that, Mick's mother cooked all the previous day, quiches, sausage rolls, ham, potato salad with sweet corn; and in the evening the front room chairs were pushed back against the walls so that sixteen or seventeen people could shout and laugh across at one another. Candy, the fat labrador dog, distracted by the smell of food, was unable to sit down and rest but patrolled helplessly back and forth sighing and bumping into people's legs until they shut her upstairs where she barked and yelped all night to be let out again. Whenever she fell silent Mick's father looked round with a smile and said in his faint, worn-out voice,

"Dog's mithered itself to death, then."

"I could name a few the same," his wife said, giving him a straight look.

She had encouraged him to wear for the occasion a pair of well-pressed but voluminous trousers which made his upper half look fragile and ill. He was sixty-odd. He had been at the pipeworks since he was a boy.

"Oh aye?" he said.

"You cheeky monkey."

Mick's older brother, a fireman, had set light to his own garage with a propane torch earlier in the year. "They'll give me some stick about that," he promised me cheerfully. "Oh yes, I'll tek some 'ammer over that tonight." He seemed to be looking forward to it. The wives, who wore long waistcoats they had crocheted themselves from a pattern one of them had found, exchanged photographs of last year's party, when they had had 'pass the parcel' and Mick had won a huge pair of plastic ears.

"You're a bit quiet this year," they teased him, and then explained, "He's usually the worst of the lot. You can see him, look how he's wearing those ears —!"

Mick sat on the floor by the gas fire and gave, when he could be bothered, as good as he got. He had bought himself two litres of Marks and Spencer's Lambrusco, and was soon drunk. I heard him ask someone loudly, "How would you kill yourself if you got stuck, caving?" and answer himself: "Bite your tongue off and swallow it." Cries of disgust greeted this. "I were trapped in a settee once," he boasted. His girlfriend of the time was a teacher. She leaned back against his chest, eyes narrowed, shy or perhaps bored, smoking a cigarette. She wore a pink plastic bangle and a cluster of thin silver bracelets. Though her hands were small they obviously belonged to a climber: when she reached over to accept a glass from someone her sleeve rode up momentarily and I saw the long hard muscles of the forearm beneath the skin.

"One year we 'ad forfeits," Mick told her. "I was supposed to eat a daffodil but they let me off it."

"Someone ought to see about that dog."

The moment you step into a landscape it becomes another one.

By September the reservoirs were at their lowest, revealing strange fossil beaches, submerged cliffs and channels, a monolithic architecture of tunnels and ramps. "Water rationing may soon be on its way," claimed the valley papers. Up at Sankey's end, a hot tarry haze hung over everything. Constant shifts of humidity and pressure threatened not so much rain or an electrical storm as some property of the atmosphere it had never demonstrated before. In weather like that you never quite sleep. Long dreams merge seamlessly with the long days, leaving you entranced and stuporous but somehow restless; hypnotised yet full of ambitions you cannot dissipate —

"We're getting the weather now."

Sankey let go of the wheel to rub his hands together. The M6 had made him thoughtful for a time, and I was glad to see him cheer up. He laughed out loud at the sun and the wind as we rocked and groaned up the A686, dog-legging past the microwave station and out — suddenly, like stepping on to a diving board — on to Hartside Heights, where tourists sit in their cars in the car park and stare across at the indistinct hills of the Lake District; and in the Hartside Cafe, where your tea comes in a Pyrex cup without a saucer, plump creamy girls with tomato-red nails bent over the old-fashioned space-invader machines, out of which came the cheerful tune,

"Poop: poop: poop," then on a much higher note: "Peeeep!"

"Bloody hell, kid. This is more like it."

The signs were good. On the way to Cornwall one Saturday in Bob Almanac's car, Mick saw two white doves on a motorway banking; and shortly after that, he claimed, a girl undressing on her own in the back of a moving caravan. She was quite tall, he thought, eighteen or nineteen, white and surprising against the tan fittings, as unconcerned and tranquil as if she had been undressing in her bedroom at home except that she swayed a little with the movement of the vehicle. "Look! Look! No *there*, are yer blind?" None of the rest of us saw her, but we turned the music up anyway on the strength of it and went flying down to St Ives in a welter of rock and roll, running headlong into the immense potential of the day, while the verges streamed past full of glorious poppies bright red and yellow in the browning grass. The car was full of new rope. We had got it cheap. Between us, Mick calculated, we had twenty-three pairs of boots. Most of them were his.

It was Mick, too, who found in a cafe in Penzance a notice which read: WE SERVE RAY WING.

"Who's he?" he asked the waitress.

130

"Pardon?"

"I mean, what's Ray Wing when it's at home?"

She thought for a moment.

"I don't know, but you get a lot."

"I'll 'ave it."

Leaning against the contraceptive machine in the gents opposite the Naughty But Nice ice cream kiosk, he stared sentimentally at the urinals.

"She was the most beautiful thing I've ever seen."

"What, the waitress?"

"The girl in the sodding *caravan*."

A few dandelion seeds blew in through a ray of sun, followed by a blowfly which blundered round and round until it found its way out again by a broken window. Above the cistern, which cheeped and whistled like a cage full of birds, someone had signed himself "Psycho", and drawn to go with it a cap-and-bells; or perhaps it was a crown —

All summer I slept in a Goretex bivouac bag Normal had sold me just before he left High Adventure. "It's your money," he warned me. Bags like these had appeared on the market in numbers just after the Falklands crisis. They were lighter than a tent, if a bit cramped, and they were supposed to be completely waterproof. No one thought much of them. Often I would wake up in the morning with a ring of climbers staring curiously down at me. Eventually one of them would smile and say as if I wasn't there,

"Is he mad or what?"

One night Sankey and I had to camp in a scenic car park a little way off the A591 near Castle Crag of Triermain. It was new and raw-looking. A line of thin saplings bisected the symmetrical grass and gravel picnic space. To one side, up against the edge of the conifer plantation, were two or three Portaloos, and next to them a small unfinished building of breeze blocks, with stacks of planks and scaffolding outside its door. We had our dinner there. Blue flames hissed in the quiet. A bird pinked occasionally from the conifers.

As it grew darker inside and the air cooled down, the smell of new wood stole out of the rafters and window frames, to mingle with the smells of tinned pie-filling, carrots and Cadbury's Smash. On and off this was replaced by the stink of disinfectant from the Portaloos. Sankey's stove, fuelled on a "high altitude" mix of propane and butane, glowed cherry red, then for no reason shot out a long yellow torch of flame.

"Christ, Sankey!"

"Sorry kid. Was it your foot?"

"It was my bloody hand."

The floor was littered with discarded zinc nails. Sankey went carefully through them in the gathering gloom. "Some of these aren't even bent," he said. "Look at that. I can't make out why they would have thrown that away, can you?" He looked outside briefly. "It'll rain tonight. I'll kip in the van."

"Come on Sankey," I protested, looking at the clear sky. But he was right.

A few spots were falling as I unrolled the Goretex bivvy in the middle of the picnic area. I woke up at two o'clock in the morning with the fabric plastered cold and damp against my face, and the rain making a noise like deep fat frying on the outside of the bag. Water had already got in through the zips and seams. I lay there dazed for a bit, hoping it would ease off; then, when my things began to get wet, leapt out and ran zigzagging stark naked between the saplings towards the half finished shed, dragging the bivvy behind me. Within thirty seconds I was soaked. Mud squelched up between my toes. Still half asleep, I had a clear hallucinogenic glimpse of myself running headlong into one of the trees and being found the next day naked, concussed and suffering from hypothermia — still clutching a zipped up Goretex bivvy bag full of warm clothes.

"What could have happened," they would ask each other, "to panic him like that? What did he see?"

For once I was up before Sankey. After breakfast we drove round the Langdales for a while but it was too wet to do anything. The slumped outline of a boy hitch-hiking came up from nowhere at the side of the road, an apple tree hanging over the hedge behind him. The storm had washed down drifts of leaves which looked sodden in the bright thin sunshine. Stickle Ghyll writhed and plaited in its bed: even from the road you could see the spray flying up into the air.

"I didn't like that car park, kid," Sankey admitted suddenly. "I was sure I heard something moving about there last night" —

Mick's mum persuaded him to take a job in the Peak District National Park.

Officially, he said, he was a "warden": but the job actually consisted in going round the picnic sites every morning with a black dustbin bag, picking up the used contraceptives, Kleenex and torn pages of *Rustler* thrown out of the car windows the night before. It took him about twenty minutes to valet each one. "When the tourists roll up later in the morning, they 'ave somewhere clean and decent to drop their fish and chip papers." By mid-day it looked like Leeds city centre again, except that there was more dogshit.

"Why aren't there any litter bins?" I asked.

"They'd 'ave to pay someone to empty them," he explained. "You find some funny stuff," he added darkly. He had a Land Rover with National Park signs.

One morning he was still in the old quarry above Digley reservoir when the first tourists began to arrive. A little boy got out of one of the cars and, while his parents were fussing about — slamming the doors, looking in the boot for something they had left in Surrey — tottered uncertainly about scuffing the gravel, picking up bits of sodden tissue and dropping them again. Becoming aware of the brown rock walls leaning above him, he walked towards them: changed his mind: stood, rocking slightly with his bare fat little legs bent at the knee, staring up into an enormous shadowy corner, full of huge poised blocks and tufts of dead grass. Suddenly he began to scream and cry.

"No reason for it," said Mick. "Poor little bugger. He were about three year old. Anyway," he said, "I'll probably see you Monday after tea." They wouldn't let him use the Land Rover after work, so he had ridden round to see me on his Suzuki. When he got outside he discovered it had a flat tyre —

Hadrian's Wall, dreaming in the wind and sunshine, suffers lovers and scaffolding with equal patience. Families from the dying industrial estates of the North East come here, drawn by God knows what racial memory to stare out towards Black Knowe and the Kielder Forest as if they were at a real frontier. Conservation teams tip rubble down the gullies. The footpath beneath the ancient masonry is a slot twelve inches deep. Four swans float almost motionless on the shallow pool below Crag Lough.

Coming over the top — it had been a disappointing climb — to search fruitlessly among boulders like melted sugar lumps for something to tie the rope on to, Sankey surprised a couple from Tynemouth. Or did they surprise him?

"Ooh," said the girl, getting quickly to her feet, "he's not climbed all the way up this cliff, has he?"

The boy pulled her down again. He allowed her white skirt to billow up in the wind, looking along her legs then grinning thoughtfully at Sankey, showing her off.

"Don't be daft, of course he hasn't," he said.

She shivered and was still.

"Because I could never do that," she said.

Later, in the Crown and Thistle on the B6342, that endless road to Alnwick, Sankey asked me my opinion. "I couldn't work it out at first, kid," he said wonderingly. He stared into his pint of heavy. "Her dress was undone right down the front." He added after a moment, "I could see everything she had." As he spoke I was watching a little girl, three or four years old, walk uncertainly at first but with growing confidence along the low wall of the pub garden. A car rushed past her on the road outside; she rocked delightedly in its slipstream. Reaching the end of the wall, she lifted her dress to show very white knickers and laugh.

Watching this performance indulgently, the locals nursed their bottles of European beer, talking in quiet broad voices about Stevie Cram. "Why man," someone said. "That's just where you get the true sense of his speed."

Sankey shook his head. He couldn't work it out, or so he said —

The lights of the Bamburgh golf club winked through a fringe of grass and thistles silhouetted against the afterglow like an advert for wallpaper. The sea went grey, the islands black: from its square white tower at the top of the bay the light began its sweep. Another light answered it promptly from the south. Every time I drifted off to sleep Sankey groaned and shifted restlessly, rocking the van on its suspension and waking me up again. We had the doors open a crack. This admitted a chilly air, and the sound of the stones grinding together in the tide. Cars lit up the interior with their headlights; the lighthouse sent in its beams.

In between sleep and waking I dreamed road numbers, M62, M6, A65 and signs: WELCOME TO OLDHAM, HOME OF THE TUBULAR BANDAGE. I was seventeen before I jumped in the sea for the first time. I had that peculiar ugly surprise you get when the experience fails to fit your expectations. My arms and legs were all over the place. I was upside down. I would be battered, smoothed off into the limbless potato shape of a thalidomide baby. I dreamed of that: then, just as the sea turned me over and spat me out half frozen and half drowned, up came the numbers again to comfort me: A591 B5343 PIRAMID SNAX A6024 B6105 A6 CLOSED CLOSED UNTIL MONDAY CLOSED UNTIL FURTHER NOTICE A53 A6024 A628 NO BRAINS RULE A560 M56 A494. I dreamed suddenly of London, and Pauline saying, "Liverpool Street was bitterly cold — but such an appetising smell of onions!" A5 A4086 GET IN LANE GET LANE M62 M6 THE ULTIMATE BAIT — LIVE SAND EEL! Light slanting through the trees in stripes; lorries like coloured boxes at the top of a hill; crows, with a black muscular stride, driving their beaks into the earth or planing on the wind, wings warped and tip-curved elegantly: I dreamed without warning and completely the gentle rise and fall, the sudden sunny dips and lifts, the white bridges and broad embankments of the roads of summer —

DANGER, OIL ON BEACH.

By eight o'clock the next morning the sun was already quite strong, baking alike the eastern walls of Bamburgh Castle and the roofs of the peeling beach huts below the coast road. I walked down to the sea through yarrow like white cloisonné brooches scattered in the grass. There I found Sankey squatting moodily by a tidal pool. "Saving energy, kid," he said. He was washing his lock-knife and frying pan. The blade of the knife flashed under the cloudy water like a fish. Later, when I remembered that summer, it was always through glimpses like this, as a kind of sleepless daze presided over by the smell of waves or flowers, fried food or perfume. I was embalmed in it like a photo in clear plastic, along with Sankey. I wish I had gone out with him more often. But he was killed bouldering on the rocks behind his cottage two or three weeks after we came back from Northumberland.

A climber called Andy Earnshaw, who knew him quite well, found him at the bottom of a 5b problem about halfway along the little edge where it reaches its maximum height. Apparently he had come off near the top and fallen thirty feet on to his back. There were no signs that he had moved about after the fall; though subsidiary injuries suggested that momentum had rolled him, flailing his arms, down a short slope before he came to rest.

Everyone agreed how unlucky he had been.

"It was a broken ankle fall, that," Bob Almanac claimed. "A broken ankle fall." He repeated this several times, then added: "I've seen people fall thirty feet and bounce."

He and Mick had been on the team that brought Sankey's body down, at two in the afternoon on a hot Wednesday. "It was a spot pick-up, that's all we knew. Someone had phoned in. Police never told us it was Andy, or that Andy knew who the casualty was."

At first they had been unable to make themselves understand that the body was Sankey's. Neither of them could imagine him falling off a problem so simple. "It were an easy way down for him, that route," Mick said. "He'd reversed it a thousand times." The two of them had climbed up and down it in their work shoes to look for a patch of raw new rock where a handhold had flaked off. They were so sure they would find it. "It 'ad to be a loose hold," Mick kept arguing reasonably, as if he'd just that minute thought of it again, "because Sankey wouldn't just fall off summat that easy." But in the end they found nothing. The rock was sound; sound as a bell.

"What could have happened, then?" I asked.

We were in Mick's front room in Cooper Lane, five or six of us, drinking tins of Newcastle Brown. People had been dropping in all afternoon to find out what was going on. You would hear the back door open on to the ginnel — with its oblique line of sunshine falling on to flower pots, dusty newspapers and a brand new aluminium ladder — then Mick's mum saying, "You'll have to wait outside a moment, she can be a bit queer with strangers," while the labrador dog barked and choked and flopped heavily on the floor by the cooker. After that she would usher in whoever it was, look at us all, and say: "Well, it won't get better for staring at the wall, will it?"

"Might he have walked off the top wi'out looking?" someone suggested; and Mick was forced to admit:

"It's as likely as anything else."

It wasn't even clear how Sankey had died. Percussion of the lower back had given the dull sound which suggested a solid mass — blood — where nothing should be. To Mick this meant only one thing: haematoma from paraspinal injury. But other obvious injuries, notably some broken ribs on the left side, had made Bob Almanac think immediately of a ruptured spleen. The police doctor, when he arrived, had told them nothing. "In the end," Mick complained, "he could of died of anything." When I asked him what the doctor had actually said, he shrugged bitterly.

"He said there was no fucking foul play. He asked us to stretcher the fucker off." He laughed. "Up in the Lakes and Scotland, the teams 'ave their own doctors. Us, we're just fucking barrer boys. I'm fucking giving it up. I am."

And he stared into the corner of the room, frustrated and resentful. To distract him, Bob began to explain to me, "You're always hard put to tell whether you've got a paraspinal or, for instance, a ruptured spleen. There's rigidity in the abdomen: is that from retroperitoneal bleeding, or is there an actual closed abdominal injury? You can't even be sure which side the muscles are guarding. It might as easily be a kidney as the spleen."

Mick shrugged. They had been having this argument all the way back to his house. "You're talking blood loss either way," he said. He drank some beer. "If unattended, death in ten minutes."

"He was still alive when he was found."

"Yes, but 'ow long 'ad he bin there? Anyway, all that useless dickhead Andy did was to see that he was still breathing, then ring police. If he'd had the sense to listen for bowel sounds, feel for guarding, whatever, we'd 'ave ended up knowing *summat*. I thought," he said angrily, "he was supposed to have been on the first aid course."

"Come on. He throws up if he cuts his finger."

They couldn't agree. Earnshaw himself arrived, but would only look at the ornaments on the mantelpiece and mumble shyly, "I couldn't see how he'd fall. Not from there." He was seventeen or eighteen, a boy with a big red face and very short hair, who had once been a punk but who now — he confided to me — wanted to join the RAF and fly fighter planes. He was an enthusiastic climber but rarely did anything more sophisticated than pull himself about with his meaty, powerful hands. "You know how you are when you see something like that," he tried to remind us. "I was talking to him all the time, as if he could hear me. I was all fingers and thumbs taking his pulse."

Later, when the evening paper reported the accident under the headline LOCAL CLIMBER IN DEATH PLUNGE, we learned nothing new.

"They're giving it out as a broken back," Mick said in disbelief.

He read out, "'. . . died immediately from back injuries . . .'" He screwed the paper up suddenly and threw it at Andy. "Broken back's the last bloody thing it was," he said in a quiet voice. "I don't know why they called us out anyway. It's only four hundred yards from a road."

Just after the paper was delivered there was a knock at the back door and we heard a cheerful voice say,

"Here's your sausages Betty. Can I borrow his spare crash helmet?"

Before his mother could get a word in Mick shouted, "No he fucking can't!" More quietly, he said to the rest of us, "Let the fucker shell out for his own fucking crash helmet."

After that everyone started to go home for their tea. Mick asked me to stay behind. The others said goodbye to his mum from the kitchen doorway, while the dog, pushing its way agitatedly back and forth between them, trod heavily on their feet. It was "team night" that night anyway; though, as Bob Almanac said, they wouldn't do much but talk about Sankey. "We'd be better discussing what's going to 'appen when some fucking holiday flight misses Manchester airport in the fog and fetches up on Black Hill," Mick warned them, "and we're the poor fuckers that 'ave to decide who's worth fetching off and who isn't —"

"Now I've had enough of that language," his mother said.

"I only have to cut me finger to spew up," Andy Earnshaw explained to me when it was his turn to go. Then he said apologetically to Mick, "You know me, Mick."

"Piss off home Andy," said Mick. "You did well enough."

As soon as the front room was empty again he told me, "Trouble is, there's no real need for a rescue team on these moors. There's not the traffic. Only reason they keep us on is in case of a big air disaster. If summat came down between here and the Woodhead Road there'd be upward of a hundred casualties to find and bring off." He picked the local paper up, gave it a tired look. "'ow much use we're going to be is a different matter if they won't give us full responsibility. Look at Andy, it's a hobby to him." After a pause he said, "Look, do you want a cup of tea or owt? Thing is, I told police I'd get Sankey's sister's address, save someone else going over there. I've got the key to his back door, but I'm not just right keen to go on my own."

Outside Sankey's cottage the trench was baking quietly in the sun, a few flies buzzing over the parapet of hardened earth thrown up in front of it. Inside, the cottage was cool and still; it smelled faintly of Sankey's feet.

Downstairs a jar of Nescafé stood in the sunlight in the middle of the table near the window, breakfast crumbs scattered around it; copies of *Exchange & Mart* and *Which Car?* lay in a drift on the floor by his chair, which was still pulled up to the fireplace as if it was March. ("No sense in getting cold, kid.") Upstairs we found the bath full of washing, a knotted mass of stuff soaking in five inches of brown water. Mick stared into it and said, "See them trousers? He got them off Bob Almanac's father, oh, two or three years since. They were knackered then — Bob's father were going to bin them." He stirred the washing vaguely with one hand, in case something else he recognised came to light; it turned and rolled slowly, baring an underbelly of yellowed shirts and tangled underpants.

"I'll just let water out, then 'ave a look round."

I left him to it and went back downstairs, where in the sideboard drawer I unearthed two building society passbooks and some cheque stubs. There was Sankey's passport, with its curiously boyish photograph taken years ago in preparation for some trip to Colorado or the Ardennes. (The wavy golden hair, brushed back, made him look like John Harlin, the "young god" sacrificed by his own myth to the Eiger Direct in 1966; but then Sankey was of that generation.) There was his medical card.

Other than that, only old copies of *Mountain* magazine. If you sent Sankey a postcard, he propped it on the back of the sideboard. He had cards there two or three years old, from Norway, Morocco, the Cairngorms — "Well this trip we got King Rat 950 feet on Creag an Dubh Loch see you, Gaz" — some of which were quite curled and faded. I found a pair of spectacles I had never seen him wear. All Sankey's things — the chipped Baby Belling on the draining board; the bits of unmatched blue and fawn carpet; the one-bar fire, the transistor radio, the stereo with its handful of dog-eared albums from the early Seventies — had a used but unco-operative look. He had assembled them, and while he was still alive his personality had held them together; now they were distancing themselves from one another again like objects in a second-hand shop. The electrical equipment had old-fashioned cloth-wound flex.

"He didn't seem to keep letters," I called up to Mick. There was no answer, but I heard a drawer sliding open. My knee had begun to ache.

I sat back on my heels to look at the Nescafé jar in the sunlight. At the beginning of every day Sankey had boiled a kettle of water to make coffee; and then, to save the cost of boiling it again, carefully poured what remained into a Thermos flask, which in winter he stood in the hearth. I thought that if I narrowed my eyes I might just be able to see him at the table. "Sugar, kid? I always have a bit myself. I like a bit of sugar! Hah ha." A fly settled on the table: rose up uncertainly: settled again. A car went down the village street. I heard Mick say to himself in a low, astonished way,

"Fucking hell, look at this."

He had found a pile of magazines under the bed. They went back several years, copies of *Men Only*, *Whitehouse*, and something called *Young Girls in Full Colour* which featured smiling but haggard twenty year olds in pleated school skirts. Mick turned the pages, giving every so often an awkward laugh; and then, encouraging me to put into words something he couldn't, said, "What do you mek of it, eh?" and "What do you mek of that?"

This reminded me so clearly of Normal that when I looked at the bright, slippery, heavily laminated covers it was Normal I could see, running about in the teeming rain on the moor at Greenfield, taking snaps of scattered children's clothes. For a moment, I could see his wife, too.

I tipped the pile over so that it spilled across Sankey's bedroom carpet, which was newer than you would expect, with a dense, violent, foliate pattern in blacks, reds and greens.

"People have to do something," I said.

Mick stared at me.

"Put them back under the bed," I advised him.

Was I annoyed with him for noticing them at all — valeting the scenic car-parks, he must see worse every day — or only for drawing them to my attention? "Do what you like," I said irritably. "I'm going out for a minute."

That evening the air was so still I could hear rooks cawing and people mowing lawns a mile down the valley; everything was caught up in the heat like a landscape embedded in glass. On a hot evening the rock itself seems to sweat, making an easy move quite desperate and insecure. Up behind the house, some children were running about in the grass between the boulders. They stopped to watch me while I tried to repeat the problem Sankey had fallen off. From a precarious mantelshelf near the top of the overhanging wall, you had to make a long reach, feet off, the whole of your weight bearing down through the heel of one hand. Every time you stretched upwards to touch with two fingertips the crucial flaky hold, you felt your whole body twist and shift uneasily: because of this, local climbers had named the problem The Torquer. I went up; came down again to tighten my laces; went up again. I suppose people had been doing the same thing all afternoon, most of them better climbers than me. "Can't you even do that, mister?" the children shouted.

Nobody I knew was up there. Anyone not at "team night" would be over on the cool, lichenous, north-facing crags at Pule Hill and Shooter's Nab, struggling with unfamiliar bulges and overhangs until sore hands drove them to sit down and watch the sun, a flat orange disc in a sky the colour of pigeon feathers, preside over salients of moorland which seemed to be painted on separate, endlessly receding panes of glass. Another day, Sankey would have been there himself. "I hate the first two months of the year," he had told me. "Well, you do, don't you?"

I remembered myself answering: "Nothing like the summer."

By the time I got back to the cottage Mick had done the washing in the bath and pegged it out. "I thought I might as well rinse it through," he said. "Save someone else the trouble." We watched it for a moment or two, hanging slackly from the line in the gold light. It was already beginning to dry, Mick thought. He would never have done his own washing, which he left to his mum. "What else 'ave I done, then?" he said. "I bet you can't tell me."

"I don't know," I said. "What?"

"Well at least 'ave a *look*, you dozy sod."

While I fought with The Torquer he had filled Sankey's trench in and stamped the earth down on top of it.

"I put them magazines in it," he said. "Buried them. Be best." When he saw my expression, he lost his confidence again. "It's just that his sister might not have wanted to see them," he explained. "Look here." He had found Sankey's address book in the top flap of a rucksack. "She lives in London," he said. "I never expected that."

The funeral took place down there about a week later.

"We were all chaotically pissed the day Doug Ainley got buried," Normal told me on the phone the night before. "I've never seen a food fight like it. I took some great photos." When he turned up at Huddersfield station the next morning he was carrying a huge Russian five-by-three plate camera he had bought a week ago. He was late, and he thought he might have packed the wrong film for it. All the way to London on the train he drove Bob Almanac mad.

"For Christ's sake Normal. Point it somewhere else."

"Click," Normal said.

"It's his new toy," Mick told Bob. "He won't stop playing wi' it now till he's broken it."

"Piss off Mick," Normal said equably. He decided that, after all, the film he had would work. "It ought to anyway. Click."

Climbers came down from all over Yorkshire and Lancashire, people Sankey had known since he started climbing in the late Fifties with the old Phoenix Club. There was a suggestion that, for old time's sake, Pete Livesey and Jill Lawrence might be there; Normal said later that he saw them in the cemetery, but they left early. I didn't notice them.

Sankey's sister had decided to have him buried at Nunhead in South London. She lived nearby. Behind its high eroded brick walls the cemetery was being reclaimed continually from a waste. Even as the service took place, gangs from Southwark council were working off the wider, less overgrown gravel paths, chopping out bramble and elder from the half forgotten graves nestling under the Ivydale Road wall. Sankey's blond wood coffin, with its bouquets of yellow dahlias, was wheeled out of the hearse on a kind of height-adjustable trolley, his grave disguised to the last with strips of florist's grass. Rain dripped mercilessly into the hole, fogging the cellophane on the bunches of flowers laid out in rows beside it like the equipment of some expedition into unknown country.

The climbers had turned up in their best suits. They were shy. Already a little speechless to find themselves in London, they were further bemused by having to wear clothes which they had come to associate with the licensed anarchy of wedding receptions and team dinners. I felt sorry for them. They stood in a restless, downcast group in the rain, genuinely upset by Sankey's death yet barred by convention from pushing each other into the grave to relieve their distress. Normal's photographs show them grinning seedily and apologetically above the flared trousers, brown safari-style jackets and kipper ties of Manchester market traders in 1978.

As soon as the ceremony was over the chainsaws started up again. In the general drift towards the gate on Limesford Road I found Mick talking to an old woman. "I came from a generation that didn't travel," she was telling him loudly. Sixty or sixty-five years of age, she had a perfect grey goatee beard and moustache. This, combined with her round spectacle frames and a pale green hat like a furry turban, gave her the air of some near-Eastern thinker at the end of his life: saintly, androgynous, but still vitally interested in the world. "It wasn't so much that we couldn't afford it, you see," she was at pains to assure him, "as that we didn't regard it as a *right*."

"Oh aye?" said Mick politely. "I've bin everywhere wi' Scouts when I were a lad," he boasted. "They feed you well in the States, I'll say that — beefburgers this size." He demonstrated with his hands. "I've bin to see Space Shuttle on one of them trips."

He winked at me over her head; took her arm solicitously.

"Mind you don't fall down this kerb here," he advised.

Most of Sankey's relatives seemed to be women. They crowded into his sister's house, where the reception was held, the old tottering about from cold buffet to sofa under great vigorous bouffants of bluish-white hair, the newly middle-aged rigid with self-control and homely as pudding. Young girls whose beautiful immobile faces looked like the cosmetics advertisements in *Honey* or *Elle* soon turned out to have been married a year or two before. "I throw a lot of frombies," I overheard one of them say. "At least that's what my husband calls them. Frombies." The very meaninglessness of this released the grotesque in things, as if the damp air were a battery charged with it. I had no idea who they were, or in what relation they had stood to Sankey. I couldn't imagine him here among them, with a plate of cake and a paper napkin. The youngest had sponged themselves as clean of life as the sides of a brand new plastic bath. In contrast, the old women heaved with it, screaming with laughter to disguise a sudden deafness; fidgeting violently but quietly in a corner with their clothes; and always making odd excessive gestures in the region of their hair.

Bob Almanac eyed them slyly.

"Look at this," he whispered. "Nightmare time in South London."

"Fuck off Bob," I warned him. They were only women, drinking sherry and eating salmon sandwiches. I didn't want to know what a "frombie" was.

"Oh," someone said loudly. "She supports *cats*, does she?" And then: "It's voluntary. Eight o'clock at the Lower Houses."

Bob grinned triumphantly at me and went off to get something to eat. He seemed quite at home. The rest of the climbers, though, wandered about as if they couldn't quite understand why we were there, looking along the shelves of books or out into the back garden with its well-groomed conifers and little stone path. They had tried the creamed avocado; brightened up a little at the cheese dip. "They've done us well here, you've got to give them that," Mick said to Normal. "They needn't 'ave 'ad us at all, really." They were staring up at a print of Munch's *Spring*, which shows a dying woman sitting near sunlit net curtains.

"What do you make of this, then?"

Believing perhaps that people should be as responsible for what they witness as for what they do — determined anyway to take no comfort from the unhinged or the immature, Sankey's co-conspirators in an inexplicable act — his sister was defiant and suspicious.

With me I had a Polaroid of Sankey (the only photograph any of us, even Normal, could find at short notice), taken that January on the indoor wall at the Richard Dunn Centre in Bradford. It was an eerie looking shot, its colours skewed by the fluorescent lighting, in which the climber could be seen suspended, not very high up, in a kind of threatening luminous greyness. A whole section of the wall appeared to be falling outwards and downwards as he scuttled across it to the debatable security of blurred rectangular forms. His determination seemed like panic. White light from the Polaroid flash had done nothing to clarify matters, only spilled uselessly off the pillar which leaned slightly off the vertical in the left hand edge of the frame. For this reason Sankey had always called it "the Dr Who picture".

"Who's this?" asked his sister when I showed it to her. "Is that water underneath him?"

"I don't think so," I said. I explained again that it had been taken inside a sports hall. "I think it's the floor. They polish it. I'm sorry it's not much of a photo; but we thought you'd like to see something."

"Well it looks like water," she said. "I suppose you all encouraged him to do this?"

And she pushed the Polaroid roughly back into my hand, incapable of comprehending how or where it had been taken; or why. For a moment I couldn't understand, either —

Some of the Lancashire quarries have no name, only a number. The local council uses them as waste tips. You struggle through the weeds with your green towelling headband, your rucksack and your rack of equipment, hoping for tall clean gritstone buttresses the colour of a sandy beach. Instead clouds of blackish flies swarm up to greet you from the heaps of domestic rubbish on the bare quarry floor. I remember Sankey turning away from the baking, unearthly walls of Wilton Two — where he would soon be confronting a fifty foot fall on to his hands and knees — and murmuring, "Not much of a view, kid." It isn't far from this kind of climbing — gymnastics in a rubbish dump — to the holds of an artificial wall in Leeds or North London, made polished and greasy by the passage of innumerable sweaty fingers, and without any virtue but the combinations they can be strung into. Out of some confused view of climbing, people always ask you what region of the Alps your snaps show; out of an idea of communication equally confused, you always try to explain why the Alps no longer necessarily play a part.

"Did *you* encourage him?" Sankey's sister asked me directly.

Suddenly she shouted, "I hate water!"

"Try not to think about it," her husband recommended. "It's just the polished floor."

He put his arm across her shoulders, but this gesture only made it seem as if she were supporting him, and the weight of it depressed her further. I was surprised not so much by their large house as their age. They were ten or fifteen years older than Sankey and comfortably settled in East Dulwich, so that it was like talking to someone's retired parents. She had been a teacher; he still worked for the Polytechnic of Central London. The snap-framed Expressionist prints on the walls were hers. ("Her idea of art," he told me later with a short laugh.) Neither of them had a trace of a northern accent left, which also surprised me.

"People do what they do," he tried to reassure her. "It's their own choice."

"Oh yes," she agreed bitterly. "I heard all about that from him. Every Christmas."

I could see her and Sankey as children, laughing out of the same bone structure, the same mouth of large but even teeth, the same black and white Kodak print with the sea at Morecambe or Blackpool a thin horizontal line in the background. "I know how we can get an ice-cream, kid," I could hear him say conspiratorially (or so I thought). The same eyes which had made him look shy and retarded at one moment, sly and childlike the next, lent her an intelligent, impatient, disbelieving look, as if she had had enough of children and childhood for good. The jaw which had made him resemble in his late twenties and early thirties the young John Harlin now gave her a bony, mannish appearance.

"Excuse me," she said to me. "I think someone's disarranged my flowers."

She walked away abruptly, looking straight ahead. At the other end of the room a vase of asters was going off like a firework in the dim mid-afternoon air, yellow and white stars and silent crackles of light. She stopped by them for a moment, then disappeared into the kitchen. The guests stared after her; at me; at the other climbers. Though I tried to talk to her again, she avoided me.

Later, washed up somehow in the empty breakfast room with Sankey's brother-in-law, I showed him the Polaroid. He barely glanced at it before passing it back.

"Interesting," he said.

Trying to think of something else to say to one another about it — or anything else — we stood by the bay window and watched the rain beading his neat lawn. It was raining that Wednesday in a long diagonal band across the south east and much of the Midlands. By the weekend it would have spread to the north. The hot spell was over. This side, the garden was large, with steps down to the lawn, some holly trees and shrubbery at the end away from the house, and a short drive which led to the old fashioned wooden garage. Three robins were hopping about on different parts of the lawn in the rain, ignoring one another.

"I don't think I've ever seen three together in a garden all at once like that," I said.

"We had eight here last winter." He looked at me as if he thought I might not believe him, then went on, "But they fought until there was only one left. Mid-air fights, feathers floating down, the lot, until there was only the cock-robin left."

This was produced with such relish and premeditation I couldn't think of a reply to it. In the end, just for something to say, I asked him,

"Do you miss the north at all?"

"I've never been there myself," he said dryly, "but I've heard a lot about it."

"What part of Yorkshire was your wife born in?"

"Kent," he said. "The Kent part. Didn't you know?" He stared at me and then began to laugh. "They were both born in Kent," he said. "He went to grammar school in Tunbridge Wells until he was eighteen, and then got a degree in electronics at Cambridge. It's one of the things that makes her so bitter. It's not just the waste of a good career. It's that he never saw Yorkshire until he was nineteen, on some university coach trip." He laughed again. "Can you tell me why someone with a good Cambridge degree buries himself away up there and pretends to be as thick as two planks?"

When I said nothing, he rapped hard on the window so that the glass boomed and the three robins flew away.

"Thick as two short planks," he said.

How could I explain Sankey to him? I couldn't explain him to myself.

"I really only came to say goodbye," I said. "And thank you."

He looked at his watch. He sighed.

"I'm expecting a mechanical digger. I thought I heard it a moment ago, but I can't see anything." He arranged much of what he said around the hinge of that "but". You saw it had been a hinge in his life — or if not exactly that, then an articulation of his way of understanding or ordering his life. "We're having the drive dug up.

It was the wrong day for it, I suppose. Anyway, he won't come until tomorrow now."

"Goodbye," I said.

For some reason I was thinking of the New Year's do at Mick's house on Cooper Lane. Towards the end of the evening, they played a memory game, which a woman with very fat legs began by chanting the refrain, "I went to market and I bought a cow." Each player had to repeat correctly what the previous players had bought, and add something new to the list. It took a surprisingly long time to play. The women were better at it than the men: at midnight three of them were forced to call it a draw, and by then the list ran to forty-five items, including a pig, a sheep, a new TV, a notebook ("memory book"), a videotape of the latest *Dallas* episode, and a cassowary. Accuracy was not enforced, except in order. Longer items were ruthlessly compacted or simplified. "Some scarlet beads" rapidly became "beads"; other compressions were "*Dallas* tape" and for "partridge in a pear tree", "partridge". "Cassowary" suffered several modifications both accidental and deliberate, becoming "casserole" and even "cashmere sweater", to considerable laughter. Many of the purchases were hit upon only after thought, or a glance round the room; others were clearly designed to reveal the preoccupations of the player, as in "fitted kitchen" or "a new climbing rope".

There was a lot of good-natured teasing of the men, who often couldn't think of a word to add; and especially of Sankey, who seemed unable to remember the other words either. Once or twice before they allowed him to drop out of the game I saw his eyes go quite blank with anger as he looked at one or another of the older women. Later he explained, "I weren't letting on, kid, but I felt right ill. Right bad." But to me he had looked like someone waking up suddenly and wondering how he came to be where he was.

13 · KEEPING HOLD

I kept a record, or at any rate a list, of the climbs I was doing, in an old fashioned foolscap account book with black covers and a spine of discoloured red cloth. Its pages were yellow and grubby at the edges and I had mended it repeatedly with Sellotape which was itself now yellowed and cracked. Each climb was entered in red ink, with the date and a few coded details — a small black cross, for instance, meant that I had taken a fall whilst leading; an asterisk that I had been forced to climb back down the pitch for a rest before continuing; and so on. I would record only climbs I had never done before, and only those above a certain grade of difficulty, according to whether I was leading, seconding or soloing.

A record of this type contains and scaffolds the whole climbing experience: most climbers keep one. They will add in details of the weather that day; who they were climbing with; and perhaps footage, so that they can tell you at the drop of a hat how far they climbed in a particular year or on a particular holiday. If they climb habitually at the harder — the Extreme — grades, they count "E points" and total them up at the end of the season. Some write a proper journal. Normal's was a box of colour transparencies. Mick stuck postcards in his, or drew a little cartoon figure of himself which looked a bit like a duck in friction boots. Out of its mouth would come a speech bubble saying, "Oh fuck, no holds!" or, "A crock of shit in every pocket."

You come home with stiff hands on an evening in early autumn and, after you have made a cup of instant coffee, sit by the electric fire dividing pages into columns with a pencil and a ruler, looking up grades in guidebooks, translating from metres to feet. Experience is not quantifiable in these terms: that much is evident. Outside it has begun to rain or a frost is setting in, and all you have done by the time you put your pen down is add another inch or two to a list the only purpose of which is the satisfaction you feel in making it. Despite that, though, when you close your eyes you can still see one of those blackened, polyp-like gritstone flakes which sound so fragile and undependable when you tap them. You can feel your fingers curl round it, preparatory to committing your whole weight there.

"What's this one like?" someone calls softly from the ground.

"All right, if you're a contortionist."

"Is it any good, that flake?"

You laugh.

"It's like a Jacob's Cream Cracker up here. Best watch the rope."

In addition to keeping his log book, Bob Almanac saved the plastic tubs in which soft ice cream is sold. He would wash them carefully in warm water, then steam off the bright paper labels. Afterwards he used them as sandwich boxes. He kept his first aid kit in one. They were piled above the fridge in the kitchen of his house in Scholes, packed with muesli, wheat bran and decaffeinated coffee, which his wife bought in bulk. "It's cheaper than Tupperware," he joked repeatedly. He also collected 35mm film containers, and the smaller tubs you buy vitamin pills in: these he used to store waterproof matches, a sewing kit, little tabs of Meta fuel for a stove he no longer took out with him. They were all labelled. It was convenient if you did a lot of camping.

Mick, who teased Bob unmercifully about his habit, wouldn't throw anything away. He kept all his worn-out climbing equipment in a big wooden tool-chest in his bedroom, squeezed between the wardrobe and the window, at the end of the divan bed with its home-made duvet cover. Some of the boots he had in there were so far out at the toes that not only had the rubber gone, but the suede too, so that they were down to the cardboard liner, which was a rancid tobacco colour. Others he had decorated. The rainbow patterns which had swirled so magically round the ankles and over the instep when he bought them (making his feet feel light and accurate, unable to make a bad choice) were by now ghostly, disjointed, unhelpful. They were tangled up with hanks of frayed and faded nylon tape, chains of corroded alloy snap-links with bent and broken gates, sheaves of outdated wire wedges worn into shapes like pebbles in a stream: so that if you pulled one item out everything else came with it, fatally intricated, and the room was full of a strong damp smell compounded of butyl rubber and chalk, dust and sweat. And Mick, smelling this, was thrown back by it like a shaman into some previous life, and boasted:

"I've got stuff here going back to when I were seventeen. Pick anything, I'll tell you a route I've done wi' it. Go on."

He knew a lad called Malc, who was a climber but whose first love was motorcycling. Malc had spent two years rebuilding a Kawasaki 1000z; and during this period he had replaced every nut and bolt of the machine with its equivalent in stainless steel. "Corrosion," Malc would warn you. "That's the problem with a bike, especially in winter. It's the salt. The salt they put down." To counter this he had had the Kawa's entire exhaust system copied and replaced, also in stainless steel, by a firm in Devon. "I like stainless steel. I like the look of it. But it makes engineering sense too," he would qualify the point; and, staring hard at you to emphasise this: "Because they make the troughs in piss-houses out of it, *and it doesn't corrode.*"

In the north, a route you haven't done before is called a "tick".

"Right Unconquerable?" you will hear young climbers say, with a mixture of affection and scorn. "I ticked that when I were still a nipper. Two year ago."

14 · VICTIMS OF LOVE

Cut a nylon rope and fray it out. Often there is only a mass of white fibres like a partly opened head of thistledown. But sometimes it will be full of dark glorious reds and blues, as if you had cut into a sparrow only to find beneath its skin the colours of the macaw —

A little girl from Meltham went to bring her pet goat in one evening and didn't come back. Eight hours later, in total darkness, the team was working the deep black troughs that feed Muddy

Brook, plodding conscientiously but without much hope into the grain of the moor, unaware that she had already been found, along with the goat, in a barn two fields away from her home. Communications were shot that night, they were forced to admit. At three a.m., unable to get instructions, an ATL called Daniels reorganised his line and began combing the slopes immediately above and below the big walls at Shooter's Nab quarry. His lads were still searching at dawn; they couldn't let it go. "Which was worse?" he asked us afterwards: "If she'd walked off the top hours since, and we were somehow missing her; or if she were going to walk off in the next ten minutes and we were the only people who could stop her?"

"It were a full panel do, too," Mick added. "Teams from as far north as Ambleside. Must 'ave bin near two hundred of us stumbling about out there. Only real danger to anyone was the fucking goat."

Two weeks later they were on the other side of the A653, looking for a fifty year old Hyde man who had abandoned his Cavalier in the lay-by where the Pennine Way crosses the road. By the time the police had got them started, rain had been sweeping horizontally across the moor for hours. Luck or common sense led them to the little triangle of oakwood north of Reap Hill Clough. Rain, night, steep wet wooded ground: atrocious conditions for a close-country search. Soaked to the skin under neoprene waterproofs like portable steam baths, they called it off in the small hours, then went back at eight. It was still raining. Mick's line, end-stopped against a narrow stream to limit the search area, pushed through the wet mist and found him curled up like a baby in some undergrowth. He had wormed his way back into it as far as possible. He had hypothermia, but they got him into a fibre-pile casualty-bag and began turning him round with a combination of body heat and warm air from "the Dragon". The valley papers ran it under the headline LOCAL RESCUE UNIT IN "LIFE OR DEATH" SEARCH.

Mick could only laugh.

"It were more death than life, that one," he said. "Poor sod wasn't best pleased wi' us when he woke up in hospital. He'd been trying to kill 'is self since March."

September is the month for suicides to make their shy, determined way on to the moor. Many of them come from the big industrial towns up there, and — unable to face another winter of domestic squabbling, or pain, or unemployment, or making do — define by their deaths and disappearances two corridors, one each side of the Pennines, from North Staffs all the way up to the Trough of Bowland. Clutching their bottles of prescribed Mogadon they look for high car parks, unfrequented paths, the shores of lonely reservoirs. Near Embsay a woman hanged herself with her own tights; she had walked out of an £80,000 house in Skipton after a row with her married daughter. Bob Almanac found her. Later in the month, called to woodland above Hebden for the second time that year to look for the same missing primary school teacher from Halifax, he caught himself crawling on all fours through dense undergrowth, knowing that if he came upon the six month old corpse it would be face to face.

"I didn't fancy that," said Bob, "but as it turned out the bloke wasn't there anyway. He's probably been living it up in Oldham since he vanished."

"Oldham?"

"You know. Home of the tubular bandage."

"Who the fuck would want to live in *Oldham*?"

By September, summer is all doomed awareness of itself. Petty whin flares on the West Penwith headlands like a signal out to sea; scarlet pimpernel hides in the neat turf of the Pembroke coastal ranges (where at night artillery fire sounds across St Govan's Head like doors banging in some row between educated but childish married people). Flowers are everywhere: but there is a perceptible drop in temperature too, a sudden sharpness and clarity of the air, especially in the morning. The climbers feel this and drive south. They stop climbing suddenly and stare out to sea until their eyes water with the glare: there! A seal, staring back! But a mist comes in after an hour or two and for the rest of the weekend the crags are clagged-in and eerie, and every clink of equipment against the rock seems amplified and meaningful.

Sunshine, adrenalin, butyl rubber: magic fuels and magic boots.

It slips away at this end of the year, and you lurch after it, route by route, the summer's sense of endless flight.

In Trowbarrow Quarry a boy from Lancaster panicked above the crux of quite an easy route called Touch of Class and fell with a groan of fear backwards on to zinc grey boulders the size of a commercial refrigerator. By the time Mick and his girlfriend had got down off their climb and over to the boulders to help him, he was sprawled out staring vaguely at the clouds. CSF was coming down his nose, and Mick easily found the open wound above and behind his left ear. He smiled at Mick. "Have I done the route?" he asked. He seemed to collect himself for a second, then he was off somewhere staring at the sky again. "I'm sorry," he apologised. "I know I'm not making sense." Mick ran off to phone for an ambulance. While he was gone, the injured boy laughed and talked to Mick's girlfriend, who was thirty years old and kept looking away from him and crying as silently as she could. Earlier that summer she had come off some stupid friable traverse in Anglezarke Quarry not far from Trowbarrow down the M6, the runners popping one by one as she hit them, so that she fell fifty feet in quick ten-foot increments, the tiniest jerky little pause between each one, until she was hanging head-down perhaps seven inches off the ground.

"This must be boring for you," the boy said.

He knew something was wrong with him. Fluid was coming out of his ears as well as his nose, and he had both retrograde and anterograde amnesia. He would talk happily for a few minutes about his home or his job. (He was a technician at Windscale reprocessing plant. "It's as clean as a whistle in there," he kept promising Mick's girlfriend. "I know you won't believe me but we keep it as clean as a whistle.") Then he would look over at the main wall, where Jean Jeanie and Rock 'n' Roll Suicide run aimlessly up like cracks in the side of a house, and say suddenly, "What am I doing here?" A weak laugh. "I'm sorry, but you'll have to tell me again: have I done the route already, or what? I'm not quite clear about that still."

"'Is brains might as well 'ave been in a bag," Mick told me a few afternoons later. We were sitting in the front room at Cooper Lane, watching TV with the sound turned down. From the set I could hear faint, tinny Australian voices; outside, someone was washing a car.

Mick's mum had gone out: to demonstrate his independence Mick had made us some instant coffee. "Thing is, he'd bin on that route before, and failed on it." Psyched-out but determined, the boy had returned with equipment bought especially to protect him through the difficulties; but had failed to place it. "To my mind," Mick explained, "he never really expected to get that far. He knew the route were too 'ard for him. So he didn't know how to go on. It always shakes you when that 'appens: you start seeing difficulties where there aren't any." He shrugged. "Anyway, that's the only way I can think he'd fall *after* the crux."

"Where was his second all this time?"

"God knows. Went off for an ambulance before we got there, couldn't find a phone." He thought. "It were never really on," he decided. "He were a thin lad, the one as fell, middling tall, wi' blond hair. Not very good. You'll 'ave seen him about."

I asked Mick how his girlfriend had coped.

"She did well," he admitted. "We went out for a pizza afterwards." He winked at me. "Wi'out anchovies."

Islands of consciousness, victims of love. In September and early October you have the illusion that the year has become confused. For a while, at least, it will slip past itself in two opposite streams. On the clifftops above Mowing Word or the Great Zawn, the tourists are zipping up their coats and going home early, and every low, tangled thicket of hawthorn is covered with bright red berries. But down on the wave-washed platforms below you can still be stunned into immobility by a summer sun. Because of this, your dreams persist.

"He'd been wearing a helmet all morning, but it made his head itch so he took it off. It's a fucking war out there this year."

After a pause Mick changed the subject.

"Normal still not speaking to me then?" he said.

"You might well ask, Mick."

After Sankey's funeral most of the climbers had caught the six o'clock train home. They would be expected to work the next morning. But Normal — still on the dole — and Mick, who claimed he just didn't care, had decided to go out for a meal instead. "You're only in London once, after all," was Mick's conclusion. Both of them had been drinking steadily since we left Sankey's sister's house. "They won't do much wi'out me anyway. It's me as holds keys to Land Rover." When we came out of the Pizza Hut on Oxford Street there was an hour to wait for the next train. Pricing video recorders along the Tottenham Court Road, we drifted into King's Cross where it leans up against Camden at the bottom of St Pancras Way; and then into Camden proper. There, the walls were black with rain, and after a squabble I couldn't quite understand, Mick pushed Normal down a basement area.

"He's been asking for it," Mick told me.

He hung over the railings and shouted at Normal, "I don't give a *fuck* about any of that. Sankey were a good bloke."

Normal, on his hands and knees among the area rubbish, looked round and groaned helplessly.

"He'll spew up now," Mick announced in disgust. "I bet he spews up." He laughed. "Go on, you fucker, spew your heart up!"

To distract them I said: "I used to live round here somewhere."

Mick was impressed against his will.

"Anyway," he said after a moment or two, "I thought you lived in Manchester." He looked dispassionately down at Normal, floundering about in the area. "I thought that was where you met this dickhead."

"It was," I said.

PART FOUR

FALL

15 · A HAUNTED HOUSE

When I arrived in Manchester I didn't know anyone. I got work in a bookshop, two or three days a week. I lived with a family in Salford (they had an unmarried daughter who worked at the Colgate factory and slept in the room next to mine: at night I could hear her turn over heavily in her sleep on the other side of the partition wall), then on an impulse moved into a bedsit near the top of a detached house near the East Lancs Road. There I had my own door and my own coal fire, and on my first night found myself, mysteriously exhausted by a winter spent gazing into lighted shop windows, writing a letter which began, "We're all cobbled together like Frankenstein's creatures from the outside more than the in — we're what other people make of us."

It was to Pauline.

"Wales is less than two hours away," I sometimes still boasted to her, without explaining that I had no-one to go there with: "All that *rock*!"

She would reply, "I'm glad," or, "I'm so glad you're enjoying it."

That Christmas she sent me a collection of climbing photos taken in the late nineteenth century. Strings of heavily-bearded men in nailed boots struggled up gullies and ridges in Gwynedd or Borrowdale. By 1920 these adventures were already domesticated, a part of the Other absorbed into the Self; now we have abandoned them altogether, like a cottage industry, and they are repeated only by beginners. On the flyleaf of the book Pauline had written, "Brrr! Looks chilly! Be careful!" Did she think climbing was still like that?

I sensed a little wistfulness behind her hurriedly-scrawled, "Best wishes as ever". But that was perhaps because, in the end, I had been the one reluctant to lose touch.

"You spend Christmas," I wrote, "surrounded by other people's assessment of you: a book about Ouida. Some Korean thermal socks wrapped in green crepe paper. Roget's *Thesaurus*." This was dishonest. I had bought the biography of Ouida myself, from a stall in the Shude Hill secondhand market.

Behind me the fire ticked and crackled in the grate. Fossils emerged from the landlady's cheap slaty coal as it split into thin leaves in the smoke. The bedsitter had nylon carpets and a modern wardrobe; but the plastic veneer was springing off the surfaces of the kitchen unit, and this had made some of the drawers difficult to open. Across the street, where builders had been at work all day stripping the mock-Tudor beams off the house directly opposite, I could see furniture piled up under dustsheets in the glare of an unshaded hundred-watt bulb. A man was working there. As I watched, he walked about aimlessly, picking up tools and putting them down again; then the shrieks and groans of a masonry drill came faintly and clearly to me.

"You wonder how you came to represent these things in someone's mind."

Suddenly I was so tired I left the letter on the table and went to bed. I didn't know how to end it anyway. Next morning I added, "Thanks for the book. We can do a bit better than that nowadays!" I couldn't admit, "I haven't been climbing since I got here," so in the end I put, "Happy New Year! We ought to meet up again some time, for a drink." Over the road, I saw, the old woodwork was being burnt: but a dusty pinkish fan remained on the bricks as a reminder of the pattern it had made.

All that winter the air was dark, with bits of sleet in it. At night I dreamed of interminable conversations between women; or of Nina, who in the dreams was neither alive nor dead, but out of perplexity occupied some ground common to both states. I would hear a voice I couldn't identify say, "She was teaching them the way they knit in Germany. Well of course knitting is knitting to me." Another answered, "I know," dragging out the last syllable into three. All the while the child would look on in silence, her attempt to understand in itself a commentating presence. She was dressed in little velvet dungarees with a bib front, across which an appliqued hummingbird stretched its beak; her hair hung evenly to her shoulders, shaped like a bell.

Sometimes Nina herself would be the subject of the dream. "I don't have soap at home," she would tell me happily, running on ahead into the bathroom and shutting the lavatory seat with a decisive bang. "They don't wash me with soap."

One night I dreamed that Pauline, Nina and I went to visit Nina's grandmother, who was recovering only slowly from some unexplained operation, in a hospital day-room crowded with women and their relatives. Swagged in bandages to the knee, eyes set in blackish sockets, she looked very much frailer and older than when I had known her. It was the hour of the afternoon reserved for television. "I was following it," she explained, "before you came." Whenever the conversation lapsed, her attention wandered back to the screen, which showed George Raft in a long, incoherent dream of Shanghai gangsters. In these moments, lapped in the faint fake Chinese music of postwar Hollywood, she looked ill, used-up, haunted by close escapes.

"I can touch the back of my head," she announced suddenly. "But I don't think I could fasten a zip."

Balanced on the arm of her chair she had open to the view a box of Roses Assortment. Nina went and stood in front of her and stared up at it. "Oh dear, I *am* sorry," said the grandmother. "There aren't any left." Nina stared up and swallowed, her hands clasped behind her back. After a moment or two the old lady hauled herself to her feet and shuffled with difficulty out of the room and down the corridor. She returned, carefully carrying half a box of Smarties, which Nina stuffed into her mouth with her fists.

"Isn't she sweet?"

This dream recurred more frequently than the others, so I wrote a letter about it, which I sent to Pauline. "I've hammed things up a bit, of course," I warned her. The letter took most of a Saturday afternoon to write. If I hoped this act would bear on the dream in some way, close it out or make it meaningful, I was wrong. I sometimes have it even now, when much more recent dreams have faded. (The little girl stares demandingly, passively up at the grandmother. The grandmother's attention wanders feebly to the television set. Pauline sits apart from us all, occasionally giving the side of the set an elaborately ironic glance, as if she can see through to the picture, and George Raft's innocent world of love and violence, Chinese-style. She searches her handbag for a Kleenex. She taps her fingers. She has all the same hollows and lines of physical strain as her mother, but they make her seem irritable rather than exhausted. She sits back and closes her eyes, her face white and empty: slowly the colour leaks back into it.)

All night I followed Nina down the corridors of some imaginary hospital in the north, filled with guilt by our condition, hers and mine, yet never quite sure how we had come to be there. By day I worked at the bookshop, which by reason of its own guilt was tucked away in the blackened labyrinth south of Tib Street.

I was on my own much of the time, with the broken stockroom lavatory. Cold air seeped down the stairs to pool round the till, where I sat scorching my legs on an undependable electric fire and couldn't get warm. The proprietor, who had other interests in the city, rarely spent a full day there: instead, he was in and out at odd hours, cheerful but harassed-looking, to count the take or have a look at some new stock. Sometimes he would be waiting for me on the pavement at half past eight in the morning; more usually I would find myself fetching his "lunch" — fish, chips and gravy — as it got dark.

In those days the whole area was still given over to street markets and novelty shops; wholesale clothiers, by then mainly Pakistani-owned; and NCP "car parks", bleak sloping patches of waste ground, sometimes concreted sometimes not, hemmed with chain link fence and the uneven waist-high brick walls which had once been people's houses. Negotiating this waste land on the way back from the chippie, I would see the bookshop sign only at the last moment, a swirl of neon-coloured paint steady as a beacon through the sleet and rain. Old men, wearing two or three torn overcoats each, gathered to drink cider or meths while they stared vacantly into the window of Nova Pets next door, where the exotic goldfish swam round and round on fins like scraps of torn polythene. Mongrel dogs slipped between the boarded-up buildings or nosed cautiously about in the road, looking up suddenly when they smelled the food— occasionally one of them would follow me inside and I would drive it out again with a piece of wood I kept behind the counter.

"Give the bastard no quarter, Mike," the proprietor would encourage me, scooping up gravy with quick deft movements of a throwaway chip fork.

"*Goo* on," he said to the dog, which looked up at us tiredly. "*Goo* on out."

When he was in the shop he made a point of taking over the till. This was to demonstrate how our relationship was organised: master to apprentice. "The trick is," he would advise me as he peeled my wages carefully off the brick of five-pound notes he kept in his trousers pocket, "to give the punters what they want." Here he would grin. "Exactly what they want, mind —" making a broad gesture to indicate the loaded shelves around us— "and nowt more." It worked. In just a few months I had seen him open shops in Bradford and Bolton; he was looking for premises to rent in Liverpool. He had a quiet authority over the customers, and after years of dealing with them knew many of them by name.

"Charge them three times what it's worth," he believed, "and they'll thank you as they go out the door." When I asked him if he'd ever tried a wider range of books, he said: "No room for anything else since Maggie got in!"

He chuckled.

"Give 'em what they want. The stronger the better!"

What they wanted was imported science fiction, mysticism, anything to do with drugs, sex, murder or pop music. Above all they wanted *Spank* and *Playbirds*; *Rustler*, *Count* and *Whitehouse*: what he described as "fun", sealed in plastic bags to make it seem stronger than it was, and to keep the fingermarks off the double glossy pages of spread legs and splayed buttocks. THESE BOOKS FOR ADULTS ONLY! exclaimed the hand-lettered sign on the back wall. "Not that I've met an adult in here," he complained cheerfully; the spankers were the worst.

"We prefer to deal new," he had instructed me on my first day. Secondhand stuff — which I might take at my own discretion, but only for credit never cash — was thrown into a bin next to the door, marked up a thousand percent; and if I didn't have my wits about me, he promised, the old drunks would have it right out from under my nose. "I've cured them of trying to sell it back to me. But you want to see them in the rush hour, flogging used copies of *Fiesta* to businessmen on Piccadilly station! Some of those mags have been wanked over so many times the pages are stuck together."

He wore a woman's fur coat — "I've had this since I was a hippy. Can't imagine me with hair down to here, can you?" — and flared trousers. He paid me by the day. I wasn't sure I liked him at first, but in the end we became quite friendly. He had that energy and ambition some men find from nowhere in their forties, as if middle age suited them better than being young.

Two or three times a week Normal would burst into the shop and say:

"Got any real books in yet?"

By day Normal stood jaundiced with boredom behind the counter at High Adventure. At night he sorted through his colour slides, or watched television with his wife. She had encouraged his interest in mountaineering literature, and now he had a collection that ranged from *Annapurna Sanctuary* and the memoirs of Aleister Crowley to a mint signed copy of *Rock Climbers in Action in Snowdonia*. I think he had read one or two of them. He visited me less to break up the tedium of the long winter afternoons than because he still cherished the idea that he might stumble across a first edition of *Caves & Crags of the High Peak* among the stained and dog-eared stuff in my bin. All bookshops were the same bookshop to Normal. Anyway, he never found anything, and always ended up at the rear shelves, leafing through *Silky* or *Journal of Sex*.

"This is some filthy stuff, you know."

I was under no illusions. I had met him accidentally. But I hoped that if I was patient he would ask me to go climbing with him.

He used to say, "You take your life in your hands coming to this place!"

Sometimes his wife picked him up on her way home from work. I don't know what she made of the shop. Later, when modern developments like the Arndale Centre replaced all those bruised old streets, she told me, "'Human factory farms' is what I've christened them." But then added, "At least they've given people somewhere clean and warm to go," as if she believed they had been planned not for the lower middle-class shopper but for the socially-disabled and uneasy of heart — all the dossers she had glimpsed under the car-park lights when she came to collect Normal, whom she still at that time called "pet". They hadn't long been married; they lived in a flat near St George's Park, but were already saving so she could move the twenty-five miles back to Yorkshire. She drove a Rover 2000 her father had owned, and it reminded her of home.

Normal was wary of both vagrants and stray dogs, especially if they were at all self-possessed. He overemphasised their fierceness and undependability, their size and dirtiness. At the same time he envied it. He was less afraid of them, I thought at the time, than of his own tendency to stray. He had, after all, once fallen off a train.

"You take your life in your hands."

"That's an odd pair of punters," my boss said one night after they had gone.

He stared out after them into the falling sleet.

A step in the street, a scuffed front door, stained paint beneath the keyhole. Inside, some wear of the staircarpet, a chip in the skirting board, the sound of a bunch of keys returned endlessly to a coat pocket. The water heater darkens the wallpaper above the sink — this can be said to be wear and tear but not precisely use. A milk float drifts past each morning — this can be said to be motion but it isn't change. The hall and the stairs begin to smell of disinfectant — but this isn't really a record of occupation, only an enigma.

"Visit a street you used to know," someone once said to me, "and you can't even remember which house you lived in. All it does is remind you again of something that happened there: something you've always remembered anyway."

Pauline answered my letters in early April.

She was, she said, well.

Work was taking up her time, as usual, but the main reason she had been slow in replying was that she had moved into a new flat. The address was at the top of the letter. She had been offered a ninety-nine year lease on an old fashioned service flat on the third floor. "It was one of those spur-of-the-moment things that always work out so well for me." One day the place in Camden had begun to seem shabby and oppressive, she was having difficulty with the landlord, difficulty with a broken window, difficulty sleeping; the next, this had turned up.

"I feel so excited!"

She wasn't sure whether she was in Bloomsbury or Fitzrovia, or some shadowy neglected quarter which had a share in both. I would probably remember the area, she said. I did. It was one of the quiet, expensive streets between the University and Tottenham Court Road. She had been lucky to get something there.

"The front room is lovely, very tall and elegant, with a shallow bay window which looks out on to a garden. You can see the attic windows at the back of one of the little Gower Street hotels. People are already throwing them open in the evening and staring across London as if it's the Promised Land!" She always tried to spend part of the morning there. Spring had come early; the sun shone through the houseplants on the window sill, turning their leaves transparent and luminous; she read all morning, Elizabeth Taylor, V. S. Pritchett, "or I just stare at all my furniture, which is completely transfigured by such posh surroundings. The cats adore it!"

The only fly in the ointment was what she called "the Pit".

The building had a deep central well, the tiled walls of which were shadowy even in the middle of the day and covered with a mass of thick black waste pipes. All the flats had at least one room which faced this well, and as soon as you opened a window on to it, Pauline complained, "to air the dining room or something", you would smell everyone else's cooking suddenly and very clearly for a moment — then it was gone — or hear their voices as if they were in the room behind you, "having some endless dreary argument about money, or an opera." Down the Pit at all times of the day and night would come a cry — short, but very loud and penetrating — she could never identify.

"Can you imagine?" she asked me. "Especially on your own in the lavatory at half past two in the morning! It sounds exactly like a peacock."

Sometimes an even more unnerving noise would float down the Pit, halfway between human speech and the barking of a dog, like an animal trying to talk. This was always accompanied by considerable coming and going in the flat immediately above hers — hurried footsteps, water turned on and off, furniture moved about.

Was it someone's pet? She had no idea. "We all hear it, but if they're ill up there, or they're keeping some mad old relative, no one else in the building knows," she concluded, and turned the letter to other things. She was sorting out stock for the Harrogate Fair. She had got hold of a mint copy of *The Vodi* by John Braine, not valuable but one of her favourite books, "and *signed*. I shall never sell it on!" She was in the middle of transferring stock from the fruit store in Stucley Place, which had become a bit too damp, to a basement in N9. "I've had to have heaters and dehumidifiers in there for a month, and a proper carpenter to build the shelves." Selling books was harder work than people supposed. "Just the sheer physical effort of moving them about." She was so worn out by all the to-ing and fro-ing she was thinking of buying a small van of some sort to make things easier. She took issue with my dream about Nina.

"Nina was never that spoiled," she maintained, "though I daresay my mother would have liked her to be." She went on to describe a dream of her own — "I had this while Nina was still alive" — in which she had seen the little girl standing alone in a corner of an empty room, pulling faces at nothing.

"I realised after a moment she was practising expressions she had seen us use, my mother and I." Converted into theatrical frowns and grimaces, these complex adult looks of anger or irony or sympathy followed one another without logic. "Her face was amazingly elastic. Every so often would come that brilliant, candid smile she could give you when she wanted something —" It was like punctuation. The effect was not so much of duplicity as of emptiness. "I suppose all children mimic their parents. But all the time she was alive I had a horror that Nina would never really grow up, and that when she was older I would see those overdone winces and grins and tics pass over her face without anything underneath to support them. It made me shudder even in the dream.

"Was it a bit harsh of me to think of her like that? It was, you know. It was a bit harsh."

She had never admitted it before. Realising this, perhaps, she ended the letter suddenly. "Yes, we should meet. I'd like that." I telephoned her a few days later, and arranged to go down to London at the end of the month.

It wasn't much of an April in the North. Yorkshire was sodden, the limestone soaked and striped like a zebra with seepage lines. At Easter Normal got snowed off Stanage, or so he claimed. He had gone over there with a friend of his called Dirty Derek.

Dirty Derek always boasted that he had started 'low down the grades' and worked his way up, as if this prolonged candidacy or struggle-to-achieve not only set him apart from the flashier Lancashire kids who had led their first Extreme in Wilton One aged thirteen, but also recapitulated the very logic of the sport. Within five years this model of climbing as a basically sequential activity — beginning at the bottom of a route *because* it was the bottom and then going to the top *because* it was the top — was historical. Derek fell into eclipse, and we grew used to seeing him like a ghost in the Stoney Middleton cafe, advising bored teenagers in silkskin tights,

"You're a steadier climber for working your way up."

What did they care about steadiness? The word 'Redpoint' was written in the magazines — they'd heard it spoken on the campsites around Buoux and Verdon, brought it home to Sheffield with them wonderingly. *Redpoint*: it was like cradling something brand new in your hands, a stainless steel bolt, or a T-bar karabiner light as a plastic whistle. *Redpoint*.

Derek washed up by accident or design in America, which saved his reputation with the generosity of a continent. In Colorado, where he prowled the Canyonlands wearing a new gold stud in his ear (it itched and burned for weeks in the powerful sun), he became quite suddenly the darling of the Boulder social scene, memorable among its scalp locks and dark glasses for his long curly hair and Lancashire accent. Once rescued three times in a day off Edge Lane, the E5 testpiece at Millstone Quarry, he now soloed The Naked Edge — a mythological act even in the inflationary climate of Normal's rhetoric, proving that while some lives flare up from the first, others move steadily towards a prefigured redemption.

When I knew him Derek had smooth olive skin and a black moustache so sparse you could clearly see every individual hair. This made him look more innocent than he was. Normal called him Dirty Derek because he was always so clean. On Stanage that Easter Sunday he had gone off to solo Milsom's Minion, an obsolete problem abandoned long ago above the Plantation. "The weather was perfectly clear," Normal insisted, "and he wasn't thirty yards away. I was standing at the bottom of Paradise Wall. I watched him walk to the bottom of the route." Snow had whirled down out of nowhere, pouring between the buttresses like Bold Automatic out of a burst launderette dispenser, and Derek simply vanished into it. "It was like the Pyrenees out there!" said Normal.

They had walked about for a while, shouting — "Normal!" "Derek!" "Normal!" "Derek!" — and then, as their voices grew fainter and fainter to one another, given up and gone home separately. They didn't bump into one another again until two weeks later, on Deansgate near the junction with Peter Street.

"What happened to you, then?"

"I got turned around in the white-out and walked into Sheffield."

"Very funny Derek."

Telling stories like this cheered Normal up. But for the most part of that month he stared — whenever the streaming rain permitted it — out of the big High Adventure display window, his eyes yellow and watery with boredom. It made him fey and incompetent. He wandered out into the midday traffic like a dog, grinning feebly at the motorists as they braked to avoid him; or if he was driving swung the Rover unpredictably from lane to lane. Trying to service a caving lamp, he cracked the battery case. A few days later holes blossomed in his jeans, where tiny spots of acid had consumed the fabric; in a pile of brand new windproof jackets (subsequently he gave me one on the grounds that it was shopsoiled); and even in some of the rope stock, which had to be written off. In the end I was to grow as impatient with Normal as everyone else. But at the time such incidents were precious hints, and not just at the state of his temper.

One lunchtime I found him and Dirty Derek, along with a Warrington climber I knew only as 'Gob', competing to see who could do the most one-finger pullups from a Petzl bolt driven into the stockroom wall. Before they located a breeze-block that would accept the bolt, they had made five two-inch exploratory holes in what turned out to be a plasterboard partition. It looked pocked and ugly.

"Oh come on now Normal!" they were shouting. "One finger!"

Even as I walked through the door there was a snapping sound, a puff of dust, and the bolt pulled out again. Normal looked up at me from the floor. He rubbed his elbow. "How do, Mike. Want a brew? Just put the kettle on then." When I took the kettle to the sink to fill it I discovered they had burned the bottom out of it that morning, testing a new range of Alpine stoves.

"Pity it was an electric kettle," Dirty Derek said.

"I think I've cracked my kneecap."

"There's a customer out here," said Gob loudly. "Shall I tell him to fuck off?"

Normal considered this.

"Unless he's buying chalk," he decided. "If he's buying chalk, give it him free. Up here in Manchester we approve of chalk."

Moments like this spoke to me in a special language, an invitation to decode a whole way of life. The brand new equipment fluorescing in the gloom, the snow whirling round a black wet crag I had never seen, the events which mythologised themselves as they occurred — one day all this would arrange itself inside me. I would possess it the way they possessed it, easily. I would deploy it without effort. Until then, how could I gauge its ironies, its hysterias forever undercutting one another into nothing? I had only ever climbed on a top-rope at Harrison's Rocks in East Sussex in brilliant sunshine in July. To me, Stanage Edge was equal with the Annapurna Sanctuary.

"If you're fetching sandwiches," Normal reminded me, "I'll have cheese salad in a bap."

He waited until I was halfway to the door then called across the shop, "No I won't, I'll have tuna and salad cream. Derek, where's that peg hammer?"

If you look straight down an Inter-City second class carriage, the landscape on both sides of the train flies past in your peripheral vision like images in a split-screen film. You have only an instant in which to recognise an object before it becomes a blur. The day I went down to see Pauline everything was dissolving into water anyway, bridges, houses, trees.

On the telephone we had agreed to meet in the Bistro Europa at King's Cross.

"It's just the station buffet, really," I remember her apologising. "The pizza's awful but at least they'll give you a glass of wine with it. I don't suppose we'll want to eat anything anyway." There was a pause, in which I could hear irregular tappings on the line, hesitant and far-off, as if someone else was trying to communicate on it. "Anyway, at least we both know where it is," Pauline finished.

Neither of us had remembered that the Manchester trains come in at Euston: I had to walk along the Euston Road, which was shiny with rain, as dark at eleven o'clock in the morning as a winter afternoon, and choked with buses.

"I'll probably be late," she had warned me. I was already an hour too early. I didn't want her to arrive without my seeing her. We would both be nervous, I told myself: I must make sure there would be somewhere we could sit.

The Bistro Europa was decorated a sort of mauve colour. 'Edwardian' fitments on curved brass stems illuminated cream panels let into the walls at intervals, but left the rest of the place rather dim. It was almost empty — one or two tourists on their way home from Australia and the Middle East; a fat man in a two-piece beige suit who sat laughing at a paperback book — but despite this I couldn't settle. I went out to the concourse to study the Arrivals board (as though it was Pauline who was coming in by train: as though somehow I had been the one to remain in London while she lived aimlessly in the provinces waiting for something to happen to her). I came back in again. A couple began to quarrel dazedly among their luggage with its bright Cathay Pacific labels.

"I'm with you," the woman said suddenly.

She got up and stood in front of the man to attract his attention.

"I am *with* you, you know."

"I know," he acknowledged. He stared up at her glumly. "I know that."

The rest of the tourists sprawled across the dull red nylon-plush banquettes, stunned by the heat, the smell of food, and the steam from the coffee machine behind the counter. Local trains pulled in and out of the nearby platform. A woman came in and sat down by the door. She looked up at the clock.

It was Pauline. She had arrived early, too. She had on a Guernsey sweater a bit large for her, a faded grey skirt and cheap white plimsolls. Her hair had been cropped short and, I thought, dyed black. It made the bones of her face stand out strongly. Otherwise she was exactly as I had first met her. She placed her large soft leather handbag on the table in front of her and regarded it for a moment — her hands seemed to be a little larger-knuckled than I remembered, reddened as if she had just finished the washing up — then took out a copy of *The House in Paris* which she began reading inattentively, pausing every minute or two to look round the Europa, fidget with her handbag, or cross and uncross her legs.

The second I recognised her a kind of reluctance, a kind of languor overcame me. It was pleasant and dreamy, like the onset of anaesthetic, and I associated it with childhood.

If I had waved, if I had stood up and called, "Here! I'm over here!" or walked across to her table and said, "Hello. Didn't you see me when you came in?", I would have broken out of it there and then. Instead, I allowed it to harden into paralysis. Though the Europa was more crowded now, and its commonplace noises — voices, plates, the rattle of cutlery and plastic trays — quite loud, everything seemed to reach me only with effort, from a great distance.

Pauline went to the telephone and put some money in it. She was forced to dial the number twice before she got through, then shout to make herself audible.

"What *is* your name?" I heard her ask. "Oh, Chris. Chris, of course. Chris, I'm so scatty. Isn't that awful, forgetting names?"

Chris, another book dealer perhaps, had nothing for her.

"OK Chris, see you, listen I'll ring you back, don't bother to ring me."

And she sat down again.

By now it was half past twelve, but she seemed more puzzled than impatient. Why did I make her wait like that? Because every movement of hers only extended my paralysis. She checked her watch. She examined her face in a small make-up mirror, touched the inner corner of one eye with a Kleenex. Bending over her cupped hand, she made the unconsciously graceful gesture of someone removing a contact lens. I knew that when she dropped cleaning fluid onto the lens, which she had transferred deftly onto the back of her hand, it would look like a pearl. There seemed to be a pane of glass between me and events; the longer I sat watching Pauline through it, the longer I would have to sit.

Suddenly I thought, It's because I don't know what to say.

I thought: If I could leave without being seen, and then come back in again! I could apologise for being late, as if my train had only just arrived, and break out of this. It's only because I don't know what to say.

The Bistro Europa has two doors, hidden from one another partly by the internal architecture of banquettes and partitions; partly by the dim lighting. They slam monotonously as you sit there in the half-light trying to guess what is in your omelette. They open on to the same platform, but one is closer to the station entrance, so that you are more likely to use it if you have come by taxi, or up the steps from the Underground station, than if you have got off a train. Pauline was sitting by that one. I managed to make myself get up and go out of the other.

Outside, I stood on the platform for a minute or two listening to the announcements — this train was late, that one early, another one had problems with its power car but was expected on time. When the ten a.m. from Sheffield Central arrived, and the platform became crowded with people bumping the corners of their suitcases into one another's legs, I went to the lavatory.

A man asked me if he could use my comb, because he had left his in Newcastle at seven o'clock that morning. (I imagined him waiting for the train, passing a styrofoam cup of tea thoughtfully from hand to hand to warm himself up as he walked along the platform in the raw cold; but he had no luggage.) He had come down for a job interview. "Me hair's quite clean," he said anxiously. "It war washed only last night." He was as nervous as an animal; but speaking to him gave me an obscure sense of relief.

Outside the Europa again I looked in through the window, to see Pauline still there, head bent over *The House in Paris*. I was struck by the vulnerability of the nape of her neck now that her hair was so short. Then, instead of going back inside as I had planned, and starting everything from the beginning again, I left the station, turned right along Euston Road and caught the next Inter-City to Manchester. It was quiet and cool; until Wilmslow I had the carriage all to myself.

May ignited briefly, then doused itself. I was walking past the registry office when after a week of sunshine it began to rain again, without warning, straight down out of an apparently clear blue sky. It was lunchtime. The bright light fell without interruption across the tender new leaves of the horse chestnut tree in the forecourt. Underneath it a wedding party, mainly women in thin summery blouses, shivered and looked upward. Would the bride come out at all now? I took my sandwich back to the bookshop, where the owner gave it a contemptuous glance then stared out across the waste land the other side of Tib Street at half a dozen drunks standing about in a circle in the rain, and complained:

"Punters're a bit slow this week."

He slid the wooden cash drawer in and out speculatively, as if testing a new idea.

"You'd think the spring would stir them up a bit," he went on. The second hand trade was buoyant, but his major suppliers were giving him trouble. "Get the juices flowing. That's what we want, Mike, eh? Those juices flowing." He made a ring with his right thumb and forefinger and moved it eloquently up and down. "Jesus Christ, look at that lot out there."

When I wasn't working I would sit all afternoon in Piccadilly Gardens — because I couldn't be in High Adventure all the time — until the starlings gathered to scrape and shriek in the trees; or wander up and down the fantastically-tiled corridors of the Corn Exchange. By half past five the streets were full of secretaries in fur coats the colour of marmalade, with boots to match. They hurried past, heads down, laughing. "Do you know, I looked at my watch and it was three o'clock!" In the window of John Lewis's, two assistants wrestled irritatedly with a mannequin. Eventually it came in half at the waist and they left the naked torso sticking up out of the carpet like a woman standing in a pond.

"Sorry I couldn't get down to see you," I wrote to Pauline, "the day I said I would. I had the chance to go to Wales with a really hard climber called Normal."

We had driven to Tremadoc on impulse, I told her, at seven o'clock in the morning, in Normal's three-litre Capri with its giant back tyres, then climbed at Extreme (then called "XS") "and above" all day before racing home through the night, our one good headlight glaring drunkenly down the carnivorous throat of the A498. Prenteg, Beddgelert, Glanaber went behind us in clusters of lights. "Normal's a complete maniac. We were on the outskirts of Betws by nine!" I described how he had eaten eight Mars Bars; how at the junction with the Llanberis road, I had hung out of the side window of the car at ninety miles an hour, suspended inside the intensity of the moment, gazing out into the cloudy spaces of Pen-y-Pass and wishing — however windy and cold it was, however much it frightened me — we could go and climb Cenotaph Corner in the dark.

"Normal took three twenty-five foot bombers off The Mongoose. He thinks he might have popped a tendon in one of his fingers, his idea of a perfect day."

I had great hopes of Normal then, so I constructed him boldly for Pauline, in broad sweeps, from the monolithic materials that came easiest to hand — speed and the night, the traditional and the new, his own hyperbolic tributes to other climbers. I felt able to tell such lies because by then he had taken me climbing at last; although hardly to North Wales. Normal could never separate events from places. Boredom lit him up with nostalgia for his old Black Pudding Team stamping-grounds: domestic, almost urbanised venues scattered across Lancashire and the north-west, many of which turned out to be memorable only for something which had already happened to him there —

"The trouble with Anglezarke," he would muse, waving his hand up at Left Wall, where the brittleness and peculiar hot colour of the gritstone had inspired route-names like Terror Cotta and Terra Firmer, "is that it really needs a group of people" — by this he meant a gang — "to give it character. You should have been here the day we bricked Teapot, on Golden Tower!"

"You threw stones at someone while he was climbing?"

"He was soloing it! Great, eh?"

That May, Thornton-in-Craven Quarry, a shallow but extensive pit outside Colne, was one of these blue remembered Shangri-Las. We went there in his wife's car on a foul Saturday afternoon. At first it seemed exotic enough. The workings were elliptical, a quarter of a mile long, like the score-mark left by some glancing meteoric collision a million years ago. At one end, where they deepened mysteriously, was a small lake as blue as an eye. To get to the climbs, it turned out, you had to push your way through some undergrowth then, using a bit of frayed *in situ* rope, slither down a chute of disintegrating limestone and black mud. You stood at the bottom of that and in front of you, completely unexpected, was an enormous sweep of slabs going up two hundred feet, so that for a moment you could only grin at one another and exclaim.

"Look at that," said Dirty Derek. "All that rock."

Dirty Derek had decided to come with us at the last minute.

"The beauty of it is," Normal tempted him, "there aren't any routes. You can climb anywhere, you can just go where you like. And you can use *pegs* for protection!"

He added: "In fact you have to."

What he was trying to tell Derek was that as soon as you danced up across the lip of that vast expanse, you were lost. There were cracks everywhere, draped like a net over the rock: but they were full of mud, bossed over with moss, and they led nowhere. You could see all the way to Keighley, as Derek put it later, but you had no idea which direction to set off in. Reeling from his exposure, we zigzagged in a vague panic from one delusory feature to the next, looking for somewhere to take stock. The pool swung about beneath us, as if viewed from a helicopter. Thunderstorms, driving north and west to harangue Ribblesdale, split the sky in half and caused us to huddle together on deteriorating ledges, all tied to the same sapling and surrounded by a faint luminescence emitted in sympathy by the patchy crust of the rock.

"Be careful with that bloody camera!"

"We should be going upwards more," Dirty Derek decided when it was his turn to lead, and off he went, slipping and slithering, swapping feet helplessly as he tried to mantelshelf on to shrubs and bits of moss. Dislodged material rolled down the slabs, gathering speed in the gloom. Briars clutched matily at his woollen hat. Normal and I found most of his protection pegs bedded in mud. We could lift them out with our fingers.

"Nice pegging, Derek."

"What do I know about it?" Derek called down huffily. "I'm a member of the free-climbing generation. I feel guilty knocking a nail into a plank."

"A member of the free love generation," I said. "Ha ha."

Up near the top, where the slab steepened exponentially into the graph of some catastrophe, the holds were flaking off like dead skin when you tried to use them. The climbing was easy enough, but I began to shake with excitement. I held the palm of my hand up in front of me in the thundery lights: I'm here, I thought.

"Keep your weight on your feet," Normal warned me.

"Let's abseil off!"

At the bottom again, we packed up the gear and poked round the edges of the pool, reluctant to go home, too wet to climb anything else. The usual rubbish was dumped there. Among it I came across a dead starling, its beak gaping and its neck extended in pain as if it were still rolling and flopping down all those broad slabs, faster and faster. The rain glossed its feathers, returning to it some of the oily iridescence of the live bird. Before we left I persuaded Normal to take some photographs of it. But when I went over to High Adventure a few days later to see them, they hadn't come out.

"Anyway," I ended my letter to Pauline, "I'm sorry I didn't get in touch. It was all a bit short notice. I tried to phone you but no one answered."

In the Manchester I remember from this time, partly-opened yellow crocus buds strain up into the weak sunshine outside the public buildings, like young birds clamouring to be fed. Every courtyard shrieks with their pitiless demand. Over and against this, in the bedsitter where I dreamed my nightly dreams of Nina (from which I composed my lies to her mother, and to which I returned in triumph from my first forays with Normal believing I would never have to tell lies again — already I believed I would never need anyone to tell them to), oblique light stretches the pattern of the lace curtain across the ceiling, the way dreams are cued in an old film. In the memories of Nina I can remember having then, she is sitting at the foot of some stairs counting her mother's keys.

"Now Nina, will you have a hot potato for your lunch?"

These are not so much illusions — or even wish-fulfilments — as encounters in a fog. Pictures with sharp clean edges, they cut you and then dip away vertiginously as soon as you begin to feel the pain. Your breath was taken away once. Now memory takes it away again, like a seagull which banks against the dull sky, brilliantly, astonishingly white, then shoots away inland over the roofs of the seafront hotels and disappears, leaving you bereft —

But if I think of Pauline at all now, she is talking to someone I don't even know.

"I love the little spines of these fishes," she says to Chris or Anthony or Jonathan: "Don't you?"

The lunchtime rush is over, the restaurant is quiet, the staff have suddenly cheered up and become human again. And there on her plate are the charred tails, pink flesh, filmy bones like the fossil imprint of a leaf.

"The trouble with eating out is that just as you're about to have your pudding you smell someone else's starter. How sick that used to make me, as a child!"

She laughs and leans across the table.

"Once I was in bed ill for a month. Everything but lying quite still made me dizzy. Reading was a torment, but it was all I had ever learned to do with myself. I was what, eight years old?" She is forced to consider. "Nine? Anyway, I could never face Elizabeth Goudge again!" She makes a face and exclaims wryly. "Oh, *The Dean's Watch*!" A waitress has just come up to the table. "Can we have the bill, do you think?"

I imagine her wandering rather vaguely home through the afternoon traffic. I imagine her staring — but only for a moment — into "the Pit" before she closes the window with a sudden decisive movement. That evening she goes to bed early, the next morning she wakes up energetic and happy. She is still delighted by the flat with its odours of ground coffee and furniture polish, especially in the mornings when the cat Rutherford jumps on the table to have his milk, and his fur is filled immediately by a reflected, tranquil light from the street outside.

"Rutherford! You're so greedy!"

With the cat purring and rubbing its face against hers she settles down to read; and later begins a letter.

"It seems such a long time since I've written to you."

Without turning her head she can look down into the street. She can hear a vacuum cleaner in another flat. What can she say to someone she hasn't seen for so long? "The weather is more like April than July." Or, "I went to Blackheath yesterday to see some books."

A line or two more squeezed out, she picks up the cat — "Rutherford! Rutherford!" — and sets him carefully on the carpet.

"There was such a lovely watery light on the common that I stopped the car." This reminds her of another journey and enables her to write for some minutes without looking up. "A whole *mass* of chamomile and orange poppies in the grass at the side of the road. I felt like gathering an armful of the poppies, just sweeping them up as they were, soaking wet and hairy-stemmed and with their petals already falling." She thinks of flower petals floating on a dark green stream in some PreRaphaelite painting; shivers with pleasure. "It was somewhere along the A303."

After this the letter casts about as if seeking a fresh centre, something fixed to pivot round: "The cats are well. I often wonder about renting a proper shop, although the books seem a lot of work lately." Failing to find it, and undecided how to end, she writes eventually, "I'm sure you'd like the new flat if you saw it." And then, at the very bottom of the page:

"I'm sorry you couldn't get down to London last month. We seem to be going in different directions now."

This letter was the last I had from her. By then, though a few pieces of my stuff were left in the bedsit, and I collected my post from the landlady once or twice a week, I was over in Stalybridge every evening. I had a new flat of my own. I painted it, bought second-hand chairs for it, fetched my dinner back to it nightly from a chip shop on the Mottram Road.

Stalybridge itself is compromised, neither town nor country but a grim muddle of both. Chemical plants and stone cottages; the Moors Murders once a month in the local paper; open-coffin funerals in the huge bleak cemetery under the pylons at Copley.

I've already described my difficulties with the old man who lived downstairs. Yet at the time I expected so much from life — some kind of opening-up or flowering, a progression from one intensity to the next — that in a way I hardly noticed him. The smell of his cooking, for instance, was irritating only because it distracted me from the smell behind it: peat moor and gritstone, brown and dusty in the hot summer evenings like the smell of an animal in the sun. I found it hard to sleep. I woke early, already excited, because I could smell the same animal alert and waiting for me in some disused quarry not a mile down the road — there were no bars between us any more. The sound of the old man's TV only annoyed me because climbing at Thornton-in-Craven had filled me with such excitement: all I wanted to be able to hear was Normal, repeating in the strange, crooning voice he used to calm other climbers down:

"Stay steady Mike. Steady now. You're climbing well, you're doing well."

Although I could easily have got into Piccadilly every morning in time to open up for the day, I gave notice at the bookshop. The train fares, I told myself, would be too high for the wage I was getting. In reality, I wanted to celebrate. I was elated. I wanted change.

"You mad bugger," said my boss cheerfully when I broke the news to him. "Wasn't that where they chopped the kiddies up?"

He paid me, then gave me five pounds on top.

"Come and say cheerio before you leave."

A few days later I did. I found him bagging stock, deftly folding the plastic envelope over each copy of *Whitehouse* or *Count* (whose publishers regularly tried to drop the "o" from the title by printing it almost the same colour as the background) then tacking it shut in the same movement with a short strip of Sellotape. It was a hot day, and as the work warmed him up he had taken off his fur coat, to display a chocolate brown shirt and matching V-neck pullover. "I don't know why I bother with this job. They'll have 'em open again in seconds." He kept a perfectly good heat-sealer in the stockroom, but hated the smell of melted polythene and pretended he didn't know how to use it.

"You may as well do a few now you're here," he invited me, conscious perhaps of that extra five pounds. "You can sit at the till if you like."

I took it that I was no longer an apprentice. We spent the afternoon bagging fun books and having a chat, as he said, about this and that. The distributors were on his back again, looking for quicker payment, fobbing him off with old stock, trying to get him to take stuff from New York and Amsterdam — "Too weak for them, too strong for us." He was thinking of changing the name of the shop, and rather fancied FUNERAMA, "though I don't suppose the cops'd wear it. They'd be in here with the black dustbin bags twice a week instead of twice a month."

We had had this discussion before.

"It looks a bit like 'funeral' from a distance," I pointed out. "Anyway, why antagonise them? You'll only get closed down."

"Can you imagine it, though? A real neon sign?"

I could. I could see it, red and green, blinking FUNERAMA FUNERAMA FUNERAMA across the empty car parks in the winter sleet at the end of the day, his new commercial instincts merging seamlessly with some dim old radical urge to confront.

"Why antagonise them?"

He thought this over quietly for a bit. Inside the shop, confused blowflies patrolled the colourful racks of books; clustered, as if they could smell something sticky, in the doorway above the bin where we kept the second hand magazines. Across the road in the dazzling sunshine, dense masses of purple buddleia hardly seemed contained by the broken walls and rusty chain link fencing. Here all summer long the dossers would lounge amid rotting mattresses and shattered glass — blasted by the sun, light poulticing one side of their blackened faces. They would wade aimlessly through the waist-high growth of weeds like old Indians fishing in green river water; or set fires which they watched with tremendous muted satisfaction as the choking white smoke rolled away towards the women shoppers on Market Street.

"I had those friends of yours in the other day," the proprietor said.

I couldn't think who he meant.

"You know," he prompted me. "What's his name? Normal. Normal and his wife."

"Oh," I said. "Looking for climbing books again."

He shook his head and grinned mysteriously. He consulted his watch. "I suppose it's too soon for a cup of tea?"

"What did they want, then?"

"Back copies of *Journal of Sex*," he said. "Half a dozen of them." He chuckled. "Do they know something I don't?"

16 · SOLOING

Bob Almanac decided to get away on his own for a weekend. At five o'clock one Saturday morning a week or two after Sankey's funeral, he loaded up his blue 1978 Marina and drove off along the

Huddersfield Road, leaving his wife lying at an angle under the duvet (which she called "the downie") with one foot poking out. A thin stream of sunshine spilled into the room between the imitation velvet curtains. In a moment it would splash across his wife's foot. He loved the feel of quiet early mornings; he loved to be alone in them with somewhere to go. "I'll see you later," he whispered, but she was already asleep again.

A few miles away he drove into mist. Grey, sopping wet airs liquefied themselves on the Marina's windscreen. A million drops of water stood on the withered dock plants and umbellifers at the side of the road. Stone barns and oak trees formed up suddenly out of the mist, while the light traffic ahead of him on the road was continually dissolving into it. For a time it was a whole world, with its own visual rules; by seven the sun had burned it all away.

Cruising between the coaches in the middle lane of the M62, he turned the radio on to get a weather report. Instead, music fell into the car like blocks of concrete: Queen, playing "I Want to Break Free". Bob laughed and wound the window down. He was twenty-nine years old and he could go wherever he decided to.

"I want to break free," he sang.

It was still quite early when he found the place he was looking for. Sankey had recommended it. Bob parked the Marina and went up steeply through boggy mixed woodland, falling over stumps and into narrow drains. The bracken was as tall as his shoulder: under it the hot dusty air had a smell of cinnamon or some other spice; there were small elegant beetles everywhere on the underside of the fronds, a breathtaking brown and cream colour. Tourists hope for a morning like this — breaking trail in the dreamy sunshine — coming unexpectedly on water, or a glade like a commercial for a chocolate-bar where the willowherb down floats almost motionlessly in a shaft of light.

The crags hung over a warm narrow valley full of rowans bright with orange berries. They were sandstone, all ramps and over-hangs: bulging with secrets newly forgotten.

Bob stood in the shade, panting.

Silence.

"Not many people bother going there nowadays," Sankey had

said. (He and Bob were sitting in the Farmer's Arms one Friday night. No one else had turned up.) "You ought to have a look, some time when you want a quiet day.

"Go up there and have a look."

Bob sat on a boulder and rummaged about in his rucksack until his sandwich box turned up. Staring out over the valley, he slowly and methodically ate half a Kit-Kat. Then he took his T-shirt off and folded it away. He found some thinner socks and pulled his red and yellow Hanwag "Crack Specials" on over them. He opened the drawstring of his chalk bag and looked inside. He unwrapped a fresh block of light magnesium carbonate, white as talcum in the sun! By the time he had done all this, his breathing was even again: he could turn round and face the crag and let the excitement mount inside him. He chalked his hands carefully, rubbing them first against the block and then against each other; reached up; swung himself on to the rock with a quick pull and a heel-hook.

Ears fringed every crack!

Some were so fragile and tiny you could almost see through them. The larger ones hung off the pinkish rock like fruit ready to fall. In some places they had stretched themselves into dangling lobes, huge polyps, massive dewlaps: ears, ten or fifteen feet high! Elsewhere they were frilled and fretted like an old tom cat's; while beneath them, and in the crevices behind them, pale ochre veins ran through the stone like the marbling on the end papers of an old book. "There's some really weird erosion up there," Sankey had told him: "You ought to see it just for that." But Bob Almanac had never expected to be swinging from one baby's ear to another high in the air on a hot day the end of summer; locking off on an ear with his right hand while he dipped his left in the chalk bag; laybacking up the side of an elephantine ear! By the time he got to the top he was laughing delightedly.

"Bloody hell, Sankey, what a place!"

He climbed in these Daliesque zones all morning, slowly adapting to them until he could pull fluidly from one ear to the next, trying out harder and harder moves. At noon when he stood on the slopes above the crag, a long ripple seemed to cross the valley, as if its image was wavering in the hot clear air. Long grasses streamed in the wind. The sheep cropped unconcernedly, then moved a few paces on.

"What a place!"

Earlier in the day, at Birch Services on the M62, he had bought a can of Coke. He was looking forward to a drink from it: but a couple of sips coated his mouth like raw syrup. Then, reaching for something else, he knocked the can over. He forgot it with a shrug; ate his sandwiches; and — to give his muscles something different to do before he started climbing again — wandered off up the valley with the guide book. "There's one or two other good spots around there, kid," Sankey had told him: "If you can just find them." All Bob found was a line of overgrown boulders. When, perhaps half an hour later, still thirsty, he returned to the Coke can to see if there was any left, a dozen half-dead wasps were crawling laboriously around inside it. Bob let out a shout of surprise. One of them had touched the inside of his bottom lip as he tilted his head back to drink.

17 · DEATH ON A TEACAKE

"I was nearly sick," he told us when he got home. "I looked in and there they were, flopping about in half an inch of the thing they most desired." He used this phrase repeatedly all evening — as though he had been considering it ever since:

"The thing they most desired."

"So what did you do with them then?" Mick asked interestedly. "Kill 'em, or what?"

We were sitting with Bob and David the fireman in the lounge of the Farmer's Arms. David was often there, with his best jacket on and his silver snooker-player's hair combed back. He liked it because on a Sunday night there were always two girls serving at the bar. They wore dresses designed to slip down off the shoulder: one girl was tugging hers back into place every time she reached up for the spirit optics; before she could achieve the same effect, David observed, the other had covertly to pull hers off. A few local boys stood at the bar with bottles of foreign beer, staring emptily at this performance and talking about cars.

Bob Almanac shook his head.

"I didn't know what to do," he admitted. He drank some of his Tetley's.

In the end, he said, he had tipped the wasps carefully on to a rock: there, they writhed helplessly over one another like new-born puppies or kittens. "At first they were *stuck* to one another. I couldn't stop watching, I was so disgusted." Five minutes later they had pulled apart and a few of the stronger ones were flying away, yawing groggily off into the bracken: the others seemed less likely to survive. "I've never seen insects so pissed!" Other wasps were soon arriving to drink from the spilt Coke. Such a mêlée developed that Bob found it hard to tell what was going on: but in the end only one of the original dozen was left, walking round and round in circles or grooming its antennae with its forelegs in an increasingly confused fashion.

"What happened to that one?" we wanted to know.

"I've no idea. It didn't look well. But half the Newcastle Mountaineering Club had suddenly decided to have their Saturday afternoon outing at that particular crag. As soon as I heard them coming through the woods I packed up and left. God knows why Sankey thought it was quiet. It's a great place though, if you're into ears!"

"Ears!" said David the fireman scornfully.

Voices in a pub can recede so abruptly and become so meaningless that you think you are dreaming. People stare comfortably into their glasses. The pub cat goes to sleep on the bench close to you; looks up nervily when they drop something behind the bar; turns round twice and sleeps again.

"That cat's breathing far too fast," Mick said. "Pant, pant, pant, just look at it."

Behind him one woman was telling another, "I get quite

passionate about being wrong—I mean really passionate: I hate it!",
firmly italicising "passionate", "really", "hate".

Mick grinned contemptuously.

"I don't see why we can't drink in the Public," he announced to the
room at large. Then he asked us: "What would you do if you had
money?" He looked round the table. "Eh? Just as a matter of
interest."

"I wouldn't piss it away every night the way you do," David told
him.

"Look who's talking. Look who's fucking talking!"

Mick got up and put his Helly jacket on. "I'm fucking off home,"
he said.

"Be like that then."

"It was only a joke, Mick," Bob explained.

"It's half past ten," said Mick. "I've to mek a phone call anyway."

He was always on the phone, people began to complain. Whenever
you needed him he was in the middle of some tale, talking to someone
you didn't know about someone else you didn't know:

"They'd bin to the Bradford Wall, see. They always go for a curry
afterwards apparently, I don't know where, in some cellar next door
to Bradford City mortuary if you hear them tell it. Oh aye, it's a good
spot, or so they say: only one pound fifty for spinach and dal and three
chapatis."

A momentary expression of greed would cross his features.

"But listen, listen! They wanted something to drink, you see, so
they asked what there was. 'Special tea,' the bloke says. 'What's
that?' they ask. 'Tea wi' milk,' he says. It sounded all right, so they
thought they'd 'ave that. But listen — no, listen — when it came it
were a cup each of sterilised milk, lukewarm, wi' a teabag in it — !"

You'd hear some tinny laughter at the other end of the phone, and
then Mick would say:

"Oh aye, they're all going to work for him. Denny Morgan and all
that lot from up at Pigshit Quarry, the whole Halifax team. I 'ad it
from that bloke who says 'heavy duty' all the time. I forget his name.
What? You know who I mean. 'Heavy duty, heavy duty,' he says it all
the time. Aye, well: I'll keep you posted. Right. Cheerio."

One morning I heard his mum shout from the kitchen, "When are you ever going to think about my telephone bill?"

Mick put the handset down and went over to the stereo. "Watch this," he said to me. "I'll get a bollocking for this now, just wait." He found a tape of Motorhead's "Ace of Spades" and put it on so loud that the little red and blue lights on the graphic equaliser jammed solid. His mum came in and roared:

"And you can turn that off too!

"Whatever am I going to do with him?" she appealed to me. "He always used to hate the telephone."

His temper was patchy.

Someone at a rescue-committee meeting had convinced him that you could drop a cat seventy feet on to a concrete floor before it was certain to be killed. As he understood it, this was to do with body weight, air resistance, and the relative strength of bony structures.

"After that height, you see," he explained, "so many of its bones and organs would be damaged it couldn't go on. Seventy feet. That's the splat-height for a cat."

He rummaged about in his sandwich box. "Hey, look! Ginger cake!" Chewing steadily, he stared out across the valley through the teeming rain. It was Saturday afternoon. A month or so after Sankey's death the weather had closed down on us, gales from the south west wiping out most of October. "A doctor told me that," Mick said with satisfaction. "About the cat. Of course, that doesn't rule out killing the bugger first time you drop it. It's just that it isn't bound to die until that height."

It seemed a cruel and unnecessary example to me, and a pointless thing to know.

"What's the height for a dog?" I asked.

"He never said."

I looked in my own sandwich box, but I had eaten everything.

"He was having you on," I said.

"Seventy feet," he said, "on to a concrete floor. If it didn't break its neck straight out. That's what he told me. They're tough little sods."

We were sitting under the prow of Ravens Tor in Millers Dale. Mick would go anywhere on a wet day rather than face the indoor wall at Odsal Top. He had temporary work on one of the "community projects" that were springing up all over the North. "I see enough fucking bricks during the week." Water dripped off the huge leaning shield of rock above us, the overhang causing it to fall twenty or thirty feet out. When we arrived we had found the low, shallow cave under the crag full of little piles of half-dried shit and pink tissue paper. No one thought of Ravens Tor as a free-climbing venue in those days. It was nothing like the outdoor gymnasium it has become since. Hikers and tourists used it as a lavatory and the only reason climbers went there was to do an easy aid route called Mecca, the first pitch of which forced its way round the roof of the cave. The second pitch could be done free, but most people aided that as well. Bob Almanac and David were still on it. For some reason they had been there since three o'clock, and now it was gone five. A dull light still fluoresced in the rock where it faced west, but the stars were coming out.

"I can't mek head or tail of it," Mick kept saying irritably. "'Ave they got summat stuck, or what? It's only a hundred and thirty feet, that route." Every so often he shouted up to them to get a move on; but since he wouldn't go out into the rain, the whole dull lump of rock absorbed his voice, and they never heard.

"I can't seem to mek meself understood," he would repeat. "I can't seem to mek meself understood at all. Is that Orion up there? No, there, you dozy pillock."

He sat back comfortably against his rucksack and sighed. The stink of the River Wye, terminally polluted all the way from Buxton, wafted gently up to us.

"Get a move on up there, you fucking pair of cripples! Any coffee left in your flask, Mike?"

Bob and David were soaked to the skin. On the way home their clothes filled the car with steam, but Mick complained he was cold, and refused to have the windows open to clear it. Instead he rolled his pullover up for a pillow and fell asleep in the back, as he often did — only to sit up suddenly as the car lurched round some slippery dog-leg on the Strines Road, stare without hope out of the misted-up windscreen at the sodden, leafless trees reeling past in the dark, and say in the voice of someone who has woken up in hell: "It's only forty feet for a human being. You only 'ave to fall forty feet to be sure of major damage."

"Oh come on," argued Bob Almanac. "Use your common sense. You've seen people walk away from worse."

"No I haven't," said Mick. "No I haven't."

He shivered, and seemed to nod off again, with his mouth open.

David, who was driving, turned round and asked me, "I wonder what that noise was?"

All afternoon at Ravens Tor we had been hearing a deep thud, like an immense door swinging to in the distance, which seemed to resonate through the limestone itself at four or five minute intervals. At first we had assumed it was the sound of quarry operations at Stoney Middleton or King Sterndale. "Be your age," Mick had suggested: "Who's going to be blasting every two and a half minutes?" Whatever it was, it left a faint impression of itself, a fossil in the rock, the sound of thunder quite a long way away on a July day. Sometimes it seemed to come from up the valley, towards the Angler's Rest and the B6509, sometimes from Lytton Mill in the other direction. But you never heard it when you were listening for it. Your analysis was always behind the event.

"It's the winter," said Mick sepulchrally.

"What?"

"It's the winter," Mick repeated. "Shutting the door on every fucking thing worthwhile."

With his eyes closed and his head supported at an odd, broken-necked angle against the offside rear window, he looked dead. He swallowed as if trying to clear his mouth of something.

"So face the fucking front, David, because that's where the road is, and get us home in one fucking piece. Eh?"

The cartilage I had damaged the day Sankey fell off White Mare Crag didn't seem to be any worse, but it didn't seem to be any better either, and I was still taking Brufen, the anti-inflammatory the doctor had prescribed for it. I had a constant slight headache, a sense of pressure behind the temples which, until one day in

November, I had tended to dismiss as the effect of the weather, or of inactivity.

November is one of the worst months, but even then you can get a day out, as long as you don't mind a damp feel to the rock. About a week after the debacle at Ravens Tor, Mick decided he wanted to have a look at a route called The Snivelling on Millstone Edge. He took Wednesday off without informing his employers. "I'll be round at ten or eleven," he had told me the night before. "Give the sun a chance to warm the crag up. No point in freezing us fingers off." In fact it was earlier than that when he arrived. I was standing at the back window watching the early mist retreat — thickening as it went — down the slopes of Austonley and Carr Green and into the valley-bottom, where it boiled and shifted, startling white in the pale bright sunshine. It was more like a morning in late December, the air sharp and quiet so you could hear distant sounds very clearly. Children shouted in the valley. Traffic ground its way slowly up Holme Moss. All morning, a delivery van had been idling in the road outside my house.

"That thing's driving me mad," I told Mick. "Why don't they switch the engine off? They can't have been delivering all this time."

Mick took off his crash helmet and unwound his scarf. Cold air had poured into the room with him.

"I've come on the bike," he said. "That's why I've got this stuff on. Hey, it's a bit nippy out: but bright sun as soon as you gain some height!" He sat down and scratched his head vigorously. "Can I use your phone? I've come early to get it over with."

As he was searching his pockets for the piece of paper he had written the number on he added, "What van? There's no van out there."

I could hear it distinctly. I said:

"You want your eyes testing, Mick."

He gave me a weak grin. I could see him wondering how I was having him on. Then he shrugged, heaved himself out of the chair and with his motorcycle leathers creaking lugubriously went to the front door, which he flung open. "Come and have a look out here," he said patiently. "Come on, you daft fucker."

The street was empty.

"It's you wants testing, not me," he said simply. "Sometimes I can't mek you out."

"Why don't we have a cup of tea before we go?" I said.

I could still hear an engine ticking over. As soon as I was certain he wasn't looking I went out into the garden and threw the Brufen bottle into the dustbin.

Mick was already on the phone when I got back with the tea.

"She's like two bricklayers welded together," he was saying. "I mean, not in her looks so much as in her attitudes." He listened for a moment — staring absently at me as if he could see through me to the person at the other end of the line — then started off on another tack. "Yes," he said, "I had a word with them the other night." He nodded and took the cup of tea. "Well they were being cagey, but as far as I can mek out it's a new firm. They intend to specialise in what they call 'high level and difficult access engineering'. Eh? Oh well, it's like abseiling down council flats, things like that. Checking for structural damage. Aye. That sort of thing."

There was another pause, quite long; then Mick said:

"OK. OK. Well, let us know if you hear anything, and I'll do the same."

He seemed disappointed. He put the phone down and looked at his tea as though he wondered what it was doing in his hand. "Why are we hanging about here, then?" he said softly. "Let's go and climb some fucking routes."

Millstone Edge: a cluster of arêtes like handfuls of flint knives against the sky, ten minutes' drive from Sheffield.

As soon as the quarry was abandoned, thousands of dwarf birches colonised its levels and spoil heaps. From a distance they make a kind of pink-brown smoke in the pale light. Sandy paths wind up and down among them under the crag, maroon and orange, the colours of gritstone earth. Quarrying started here again briefly and illegally in 1983; then someone dumped a car in one of the bays near the Sheffield Road — burned out and upside down among the birches, it looks somehow as sad and vulnerable as a dead animal.

Further in, morning light strikes obliquely across the very tops of the vertical walls. From the ground this makes them seem like pages turned down in some huge book: but as soon as you get up there, a hundred feet of rope trailing sadly out behind you in the cold wind, you find only dust, great meaningless holes, layers of rotting stone constructed like a cheap chest of drawers —

"If you don't like it you can always pull it out and throw it away," Mick advised me, as I struggled with the last few feet of a climb called Lotto.

"Very funny, Mick. Mick, I can't do this."

"Yes you can, you wimp. That's not the 'ard part. You've done the 'ard part."

I hauled myself over the top. My legs were shaking.

"Well I'm never doing it again!"

Mick followed absent-mindedly, singing to himself. "You're getting a bit better," he admitted at one point. "Not much, but a bit."

By mid-day the quarry had warmed up, so he went over to the bottom of the Great Slab and put his magic boots on. Overnight, he had drawn a union jack on one of them with red and blue felt-tip pens. He looked at it critically. "I wish I 'adn't done that now. I were bored."

The slab was out of the sun; a bit greasy; polished, even along the less popular lines. After fifty or sixty feet it reared up into a dark steep headwall. Mick looked at it doubtfully and shivered. The Snivelling — originally named The Snivelling Shits, after a Punk band of its day — streamed out above him, a series of minute scratches on the rock. He would have to solo it: good protection turns up on that route, but only after the difficulties are over, when you don't need it. "They always look steeper than they are," he said: "Slabs." After a moment, he chalked his hands, tightened his boots; he chalked his hands again. Then he lurched up over the short lip and on to the slab. "Me feet hurt already!" he complained. But he made steady progress — mainly by high, balancey steps and fingertip stretches — until he was about twenty-five or thirty feet up. There, an iron rugosity like a razor blade tore the side off his left index fingernail.

"Bugger!"

Blood ran down his arm.

He laughed.

"I'm stuck now," he said. "I can't use that finger."

First he decided to jump off. Then he decided to have another try at going up. Then he decided to jump off again.

"It isn't far," he said.

He was waiting for me to say something.

"I've jumped that far before," he reminded me.

"OK," I said, in as encouraging a tone as I could manage.

Nothing is worse than being stuck on a slab. You can stand there for a long, long time before you fall. You feel as if you've been abandoned, even if your friends are thirty feet away. Mick couldn't go up: the holds were little more than patches of rock a different colour or texture to the rest, and blood had made his fingers too slippery to use them. If he didn't jump, friction would hold him in place, but only until his ankles tired. Already, lateral torsion would be twisting his boots imperceptibly but steadily off the rock. Privately I had visions of his shin bone, popped out of the ankle joint and sticking through the side of his leg in the winter sunshine, as white as the mist that morning. I ran around underneath him, clearing the bigger stones from where he would land.

"Whatever you think," I said.

But he had already delayed fatally. He couldn't make himself do it.

"Oh fuck. Fetch a rope, Mike."

"Will you be all right there while I get it?"

He stared miserably ahead.

"Mike, just get a move on."

I tied on to a nine-mil rope we had been using earlier in the day and went up the right hand edge of the slab as fast as I dared. "Hang on," I called. "I'm on my way. Stay steady." It felt strange to have to say this to someone so much more experienced and skilful than me.

Mick laughed.

"Don't kill yourself rushing about like that," he said. "Or we'll both look like tits."

At the top of the slab I traversed left to get above him; but nerves made me belay too soon, and the rope spilled down ten feet out of his reach. "Hang on," I said. I thought I might be able to twitch it across to him. Nothing. I tried again. It was still three feet away. He stared at it out of the side of his eye: he didn't dare grab at it, for fear of losing his balance. His ankles were buckling, and I could see him beginning to lose his nerve.

"Be steady," I said calmly, trying to get off the belay. "You're still OK."

"Christ, Mike, don't be a pillock," he pleaded.

"You'll be OK," I said.

"Mike! I can't wait! Look, don't bother with all that, I'm jumping off, I can't wait —"

He looked down.

"No I'm not," he said quickly.

He had to stand there in the middle of nowhere — marooned, pigeon-toed, and trying not to shiver — for another minute before I got my knots undone, moved into position above him, and dropped him the end of the rope.

Later he would laugh and claim: "The worst thing were the pain of those fucking boots!" But on the ground under Great Slab, he was in a foul mood, with me and everything else. "You want to learn to tie knots a bit quicker, you do," he said. He threw his boots into his bag, and kicked out at it. I tried to put a piece of Elastoplast on his finger. It looked raw where the nail had peeled off, but it had already stopped bleeding and it wasn't much of an injury unless you had been psyched-out by a 6a slab. "Oh shit," he said. "I really wanted that route. I wanted it that bad I could smell it." He got his flask out and unscrewed the top. His hands were shaking. "Now I've spilt that fucker," he said viciously. He looked over his shoulder at Great Slab. Suddenly he jumped to his feet.

"Mick —"

"Don't say anything to me. Not a fucking thing," he warned.

He turned his back, and, hopping from foot to foot, dragged the magic boots on again. He was shaking so hard he could hardly tie their laces. Without a word, he levered himself on to The Snivelling and climbed neatly and carefully, without slowing down or stopping, to the top of it. There, he waved his arms disconnectedly in relief. He let out a shout of triumph which made his face seem distorted and animal-like: I understood that Mick went climbing only to release this expression from himself. What it represented I had no idea. For a moment though I was awed, and almost as excited as he was.

"You bastard!" I called up gleefully. "Mick, you bastard!"

"It's death on a teacake, that route," he said. "Death on a teacake."

Shortly afterwards it started to rain. We packed our gear and left. Mick pushed the black and yellow Suzuki up past Higgar Tor and then turned north-west on to the single-track road under Stanage Edge. There, with the rain flying into our faces and the wind snatching at the rucksack on my back, he first accelerated furiously, then slowed down to walking pace, gazing at the rocks and allowing the machine to yaw from side to side of the empty road. Eventually he stopped and switched the engine off. The rocks were melted and equivocal in the dull light. Filmy curtains of rain drifted across the shallow valley that slopes away in front of them towards Bamford Moor. I could smell sheep, dead ferns, tussock grass, water standing on peat. Mick took his helmet off.

"I've had it with this lot," he said.

He was sick of the Peak District: he was sick of gritstone. It was always wet. "It looks like a sodden cardboard box when it's wet," he said. It looked to him exactly like a cardboard box collapsing in the rain, and he was sick of it.

"Just look. Just look."

Because he found it so painful to admit this, and because I couldn't think of any helpful response, I said:

"It's a bit brighter over towards Burbage."

"Oh fuck off, Mike."

He started to put his helmet on again.

Then he said, "I've got a new job. It's work away from home."

He shrugged and looked up at Stanage, where low cloud was roiling over the Plantation, softening further the edges of the Wall End and Tower buttresses. "I'm not right keen on that," he admitted, "but what else can I do? There's money in it, and I'm fed up here. And you can't just hang around all your life, Mike. You can't. What? Oh, two weeks time. I start down in Birmingham."

I had to think for a moment.

"It depends what you mean by hanging around," I said.

I was trying to make out the line of Archangel in the mist.

I still see Mick. He was promoted rapidly, and now runs his own team, mostly ex-climbers, mostly from the north. Their work takes them all over Britain. The concept "difficult-access civil engineering" embraces everything from core-sampling the piers of a motorway bridge to cleaning the inside of some of the windows in the Barbican complex, which architecture has placed out of the reach of traditional methods. For a time Mick even operated offshore, abseiling down the vast steel legs of oil platforms in the North Sea — until one afternoon, working the "splash zone" without a wet suit, he found himself in the leading edge of hypothermia and forgot how to work the Jumars that would get him out again. But most of the work is done on behalf of the inner-city councils, who find increasingly that tower blocks put up by their predecessors during the Fifties and Sixties are falling apart; and so he is often in London.

"They're fucking appalling places to live," he often says of the blocks. "Especially Glasgow and Birmingham."

Then he shrugs.

"But what they 'ad before was no better."

Food still obsesses him: he will still open a conversation as he used to out on the crag, by describing what he had to eat the night before.

"Fucking hell, Mike, you should 'ave bin there. It were a place called the Green Frog. (Or was it just the Frog? I don't rightly remember: anyway, summat in French.)" Soon you discover that he ate steak in cracked pepper sauce at La Grenouille; with a starter of ham and cheese in choux pastry and a gooseberry sauce, and followed by rum and Belgian chocolate mousse.

"Thirty notes each for that, Mike. Not bad, eh? Thirty notes!"

He wears an Armani suit.

Mick's stories about his job are mixed with sentimental memories of "the rescue", preserved in — and intricated with — an even older level of material from his school days. He often seems to forget I wasn't there when this childhood sediment was laid down. His tenses saw violently back and forth as he tries to unearth what he wants. It isn't only that the various strata have contorted and compacted together during the upheavals of his life: in addition he sees us both as exiles, and he has elected me to the oral tradition not just of the climbers but of the valley as well. "The worst thing ever," he will say, "was when I were fast in that really small school blazer. No, wait, don't laugh: I'm wedged so fast in it I 'ave to chop meself out wi' an axe! You must remember!" He scratches his head. "Were it at the jumble sale, that?" A moment later he will be explaining again why he gave up the offshore work:

"I sat there at the end of three hundred feet of static rope, soaked to the skin, wondering what these things in my 'ands were for. Meanwhile the spotter's calling down to me, 'Are you OK?' Dickhead.

"I were as good as dead that day," he will say. "It's fucking cold is the North Sea."

There's a pause, in which he allows you to contemplate this. Then he adds:

"Still, it's not the risk that gets you down."

Neither is it the brutality of the work, which is at least similar to that of hard climbing. For Mick it is simply that he has to live from week to week in boarding houses, make up his own sandwiches in the morning, drive five hundred miles overnight to get to the next job; that he sees, for the most part, only the centres of cities, the windy spaces of air where dirty bits of paper blow between the tower blocks; that he gets home to the valley once a month if he's lucky, and then because he is self-employed must spend all his free time arguing with the National Insurance people at Crown House in Huddersfield.

The last time we met it was to go for something to eat. He wanted me to try a restaurant in Chinatown. He'd been there before, he said, and it was good.

"You know, they mek you use chopsticks, and the waitresses smash the bean curd and shrimps down in front of you so hard it goes all over your shirt."

We laughed.

"'Can we 'ave some Dim Sum?'" he mimicked himself. And then the waitress:

"'No.'"

When I met him at the restaurant, though, he seemed less amused. "I'm not sure this is the one after all," he said. The staff made us wait for twenty minutes in a draughty lime-washed passage until a table became vacant. "They're all called Fuck Something," Mick said, staring at the dirt growing like fur round the passage doorway: "These places." When we were finally allowed in he begged me, "Just don't order anything looking like a garden pond that's bin left too long." A family of London Chinese were taking photographs of one another at a table nearby; every time a flash unit went off, Mick winced. "Not while that kiddie's screaming like that, anyway," he said. "I 'ad the odd drink this afternoon."

He stared round the walls.

"I can't stand these pictures in boxes, can you? Everything's so little in them."

He ordered a lot of food but hardly touched most of it. "'Ave some of this sea-bass," he kept urging me. "Try these prawns." He would watch me carefully as I ate the first few mouthfuls, to make sure I was enjoying it; say, "It's good that, isn't it?"; then lean back in his chair and peer out of the window. The glass had a dense pattern of roses on it: this had the effect of smearing and spreading the neon signs outside. Mick seemed to be trying to identify the vague figures coming and going in the street.

"I always think I'm going to see someone I know."

He drank some more Tiger beer and studied the label of the bottle.

"Sometimes I even miss Normal," he said.

He laughed.

Chalk up.

Pause for a moment. Your desire for excitement itself makes you excited.

Intention tremors tighten your calf muscles.

The psychological window is closing. If you go too soon your determination will eat itself. If you go too late you will feel it all run out of you like water.

Suddenly, you clamp your fingers down very hard on the holds and fling yourself at the sequence. You believe, as you make the first move, that you have already accepted the potential fall.

Pull up, lock off, bring the toe of your left boot up into a pocket. Reach very high with the left hand so that your fingers, stiff and trembling with effort, slot behind the upside-down lip of a flake. Pulling outwards on that while you let your weight swing right, bend the left arm until you can begin to raise your body, get the other hand in the same place, and finally run both feet up the wall until your knees are tucked up near your waist. Almost at the limit of tolerance now, straighten the legs explosively and *jump* for the top.

At this point, fear and excitement are indistinguishable from one another: together, they are indistinguishable from joy.

I couldn't settle.

November moved into December. The view was good until you came close to it: every stone wall, every tree in the valley was covered with thick green lichen, cold, streaming wet. Mick left for his new job, and shortly afterwards we had the first snow up on the moor, a short damp fall that lasted a day. Two weeks of clear sky followed; morning frosts which guaranteed a little warm, wan sunshine for two hours in the middle of the day. There were distinct shadows on the road by the church, lines of washing at the backs of the houses, threads of chimney smoke in the illuminated air. "I haven't seen the buses so crowded!" people said to one another in surprise. Ordinary life had become graceful and festive to them. "In nice weather like this everyone goes out to buy something." On their way back from town they laughed at the young turkeys growing up in wire cages behind the farms in Oldfield — white now, much bigger, standing proudly among heaps of moulted juvenile feathers.

My knee had begun to hurt again, and it felt stiff when I got out of bed; but effort seemed to ease it, so I took increasingly to the rocks behind Sankey's house. There, a cheerful lad called "Red Haired Neil" to distinguish him from some other Neil who no longer lived locally, showed me how to solo with a Sony Walkman.

"Go on. Try it. Here."

It was like discovering electricity.

"The big hazard at this crag is still falling in the dogshit," said Neil; but as long as I had the Walkman on I was invulnerable. I could thrive on risk. I played Bryan Adams, "Straight From the Heart": my intuition astonished me. I played Bruce Springsteen, "Ramrod": problems succumbed so easily I was filled with energy. I played ZZ Top, "Deguello": my aggression seemed endless. The music fell obliquely across the rock, illuminating it like a new wavelength of light to reveal brand new ways of climbing. It was still possible to be outfaced: but, burning magic fuels, I would know the end of the day had come only when my fingers let go of their own accord: I would look up suddenly, dazed with fatigue, adrenalin and rock-and-roll, to see headlights sweeping down Holme Moss and into the valley. My arms were grey with cold, the elbow joints painful from repeated pulling up, the fingertips sore and caked with chalk. Only then would I change back into my Nike shoes, turn the music up louder to combat a sudden sense of depression, and, shivering, walk down past Sankey's cottage where the FOR SALE board had been up for a month.

I never saw anyone viewing it.

The front room curtains were down and all his furniture had gone: but you could see scattered across the bare floor the Subaru catalogues he had been poring over the month he died.

Towards the end of that fortnight the weather became strange and undependable. Above the Holme Moss transmitter you could see alternating bands of weak sunshine and low thick cloud; shifts of pressure pumped them down from the plateau one after the other to give first a cold wind then a blue sky that seemed warmer than it was. Resting for a moment at the top of some problem, I would watch the late sun burning the bare trees and mill chimneys, igniting the windows of the double-glazed barn-conversions all the way to Greenfield. One minute things swam in light; the next they were flat and wintered, ordinary.

"It cuts like a knife," whispered the Walkman: "But it feels so right."

By now my leg ached all the time. At about two o'clock on a Thursday afternoon — in one of those lenses of warmth and sunshine, with the Walkman turned up full so that energy and excitement flooded up inside me from moment to moment — I made a high step on a problem I had done a dozen times before. Something seemed to lurch inside my knee, like a small animal trying to escape. I was twenty-five feet off the ground. A bit desperately, I threw my weight on to that leg and tried to stand up. Nothing happened, except that the headset of the Walkman came off and dangled on its wire in front of me, so that I stepped on it. The knee wouldn't straighten. I tried to reverse the move, but I was already falling. Each time I hit something on the way down I thought, "That's my shoulder, but it's OK," or "That's my foot, but it's OK." I could hear myself saying, "Christ! Christ!" I finished up in the heather under the climb, where the ground sloped away suddenly enough to absorb most of my momentum, with a sprained ankle and a few bruises. The sun had gone in. I was shaking. I could hear the motor of the Sony turning over creakily: and Mick's clear voice in my head advising me,

"You're not fit to be allowed out on your own, you incompetent wazzock."

Fluid swelled the ankle, crushing the soft tissues until they blackened. I could still get about on it, but my knee would lock unexpectedly. I sat in the house for a week watching TV with the sound turned down and the Walkman turned up until it hurt my ears, trying to infer the news from jumbled footage of tanks and elder statesmen, the weather from the weatherman's smile. High winds and rain were forecast until the New Year. Sometimes the moves I had done recently would pass before my closed eyes. Or I would hear jackdaws, and see with sudden heartbreaking clarity some crag in the summer sunshine: Hen Cloud, Bwlch y Moch, Beeston Tor.

"You can't be 'more or less' lost," I remembered someone saying.

You're either lost or you aren't. It was nearly Christmas. So I telephoned Normal and asked him: "I wondered if you were getting out much?

"Climbing, I mean."

19 · EACH SMALL SUICIDE

Normal seemed quite pleased to hear from me. He was getting out again a bit at weekends, with a loony bugger called Stox. "You'll have seen him before," Normal said: I would probably recall Stox jumping repeatedly off a route in Cheedale and into a tree, one Sunday at the end of April.

"Remember?"

I did. April, Cheedale: climbers under every wall, and a mass of white, sweet-smelling flowers on every ledge. The sun takes time to come round to the true left bank of the Wye. The Sidings, the Embankment, everything upriver of the old railway tunnel remains cold and unwelcoming long after people have begun to do their trapeze acts on Moving Buttress and Two Tier. Kicking his heels underneath the superseded aid climbs of the Embankment, Stox had soloed as far as the crux of a new 6b, discovered he couldn't get down again, and simply jumped for the nearest tree. The sensation had proved so enjoyable that he climbed straight back up and sampled it again, this time giving out a long, whooping call to attract people's attention as the tree whipped backwards and forwards under his weight. So much energy; so much delight in

205

himself! Watching from the jungle underneath Mad Dogs & Englishmen, as he climbed and jumped, climbed and jumped, I had fallen so in love with those sudden gibbon-like swoops — that total commitment to the air — that I felt sad when he grew bored and went away.

"I wondered who he was."

"Well now you know," said Normal. "He's seriously disturbed, is Stox."

"Really?" I said ironically. But Normal had more to tell.

Stox was eighteen or nineteen years old but looked much older, a small, powerful, sinewy climber with very short hair. Outdoor work had thickened his fingers, thinned and hardened his face. He gave you a direct look when he spoke, as if he didn't think much of you — or at any rate hadn't yet made up his mind — but it was often tempered with sly humour. His family were Catholics: by the age of sixteen he had already spent three months at a detention centre, for some juvenile crime they didn't talk about. He had got his Asian girlfriend pregnant when they were seventeen — "She's nice," Normal said. "Very nice." — and now they lived with their son on a weatherbeaten housing estate near Hyde in Cheshire. Since he came out of the detention centre he had earned his living as a steeplejack — he called it "jacking" — a trade by which, even at his age, and in 1984, he could earn between four and five hundred pounds a week: but he didn't care about the money, which, Normal claimed, he spent on stock-car racing, bar-fights, and expensive suits: the real reason he did it was the danger. Before he got into rock climbing he had been an amateur boxer. As a boy he had longed to be a stunt man.

"The problem was," Normal told me, "he thought they *did* the things you see in films."

Stox's first stunt involved the family Austin (which he was subsequently to write off on the A57 "Snake", two days after he took his driving test). He came home from school to find some of his brothers reversing it over one another outside the garage. They were lying longitudinally, so that the wheels passed them on either side. "You wimps," Stox told them; and, after some loudmouthing and psyching-up, stretched himself directly across its path.

206

"What happened?" I asked.

"It stalled," Normal said, "luckily. He should be in a straitjacket."

This was Normal's highest accolade.

Since then, Stox had enjoyed many adventures, perhaps the most characteristic of which was also the most recent. He told us about it on the way to Rothwell Sports Centre, which sticks up suddenly out of muddy fields somewhere near Wakefield. We rarely used Rothwell. Odsal Top was more convenient for the Huddersfield climbers. Stox lived close to Sid's Sports in Stalybridge. Normal, though, fancied a change. He had managed to borrow his wife's car, and drove it with random gusto through the flat agricultural land east of Wakefield. I was so used to moors and gritstone walls that I found the hedges and red-brick farmhouses quite strange and nostalgic. Normal must have felt something of the same.

"I haven't been here for years!" he said. "Great, eh? It's like a real trip out!"

Stox looked at me and winked.

"Wakefield," he said. "Vineyard of the North."

"What's it like, being a steeplejack?" I asked him.

"Well, I'll tell you," he said. "I've been so scared I couldn't shit."

In early December, lightning had blown eight square feet out of the 380-foot Shell Oil stack at Sale, then run down the lightning conductor into the chimney itself. Most of the damage was about ten feet from the top, but after Stox and his foreman had taken a video camera inside, they decided to rebuild with brick the whole of the last sixty feet.

Inside, the stack was freezing cold, misty with condensation; water ran down the bricks, and all you could hear was the electric hum of the power-climbers as they took the inspection cradle down two 8mm steel cables in the pitch dark. "It was well eerie in there," said Stox. "Well eerie." Outside, they had problems with the weather. Snow plastered itself on to the stack, then kept falling on them in great sheets; and as they went up and down the ladders, carrying rolled alloy joists to anchor the outside cradle, they could hear the wind rushing towards them across the dark Cheshire Plain.

"What do you *do* in a high wind?" Normal wanted to know.

"Hang on," said Stox laconically. "You can hear the ladders rattle." He gave us his sly, cocky grin. "It's not like climbing," he said. "You have to have a bit of a head for heights."

He gazed pensively at the landscape for a moment, then leaned forward and said to Normal:

"These Rovers'll go faster than this, you know."

The most nerve-racking thing about steeplejacking, for most jacks anyway, he explained, was moving about at the top of a stack. It exhausted you. Shell Oil at Sale was thirty-five feet in circumference and a foot wide, with a steel capstone in bolted sections. If you could make yourself look down, you would see the chimney tapering in towards its base, like something out of a Tom & Jerry cartoon. Crushed by this exposure, most of the jacks couldn't stand upright at all, but had to crawl round *à cheval*, with their legs hanging over the sides.

"It helps if you're stoned," Stox maintained, fumbling in the pockets of his leather jacket.

"Speaking of which, let's have a roll-up."

Ostentatiously, Normal wound down his window.

"Piss off Normal," said Stox. "Anyway, eventually they get the outside cradle working and start using it to look at the damage under the cap." Climbing ladders at half past three in the afternoon, Stox had seen the outside cradle coming down past the blow-out, which was about fifteen feet to his right. "If it'd been earlier in the day, I'd have been a bit sharper. I could hear the wind about to hit, but I didn't put the two things together. The cradle took me clean off. Bastard." He contemplated this. "Three hundred and sixty-odd feet," he said, picking a shred of Old Holborn off his lower lip.

He considered the implications.

"What can you do?" he said, with the air of someone stating some more general problem.

What he had done was to grab one of the trail-cables, wrap his arm round it and, dangling above the abyss, start shouting as loud as he could.

"I was too scared even to shit myself."

Eventually the other jacks heard him, pulled him into the cradle, and took him to the top. As you stood on the edge of this huge black

208

hole, he said, the refinery flares were plumes of orange flame five hundred yards away in the growing darkness. Further out were the housing estates, with their kitchen lights coming on. Further still, you could pick out the constant stream of headlights on the M62. And if you looked north-east you might see Manchester. "I couldn't stop laughing. You can't, can you? What's this Rothwell wall like then, Normal? Anything good on it?"

He threw the glowing end of his roll-up out of the window past Normal's ear.

"Anything good high up?"

"One of the things I really like about Stox," Normal had told me on the phone earlier in the day, "is this theory he's got that all sports centres are the same one. You just drive to different entrances, in Bradford, Leeds, Stalybridge."

Certainly they're all made of the same ashy grey brick; they have the same low, square-cut corridors; the same plump girls with cropped blonde hair and powerful legs, who carry their badminton rackets in identical maroon plastic holdalls. They have the identical sign on the door of the facility you want: DO NOT ENTER UNTIL YOUR ALLOTTED TIME, with the same vague purgatorial implications. The air in them is dusty and too hot, and when you get to the wall, the winter has driven in the same lot of rock-climbers, who smell of sweat and chalk and look like a hundred dull migratory birds on the banks of the same grey estuary. A shared eccentricity is quite soon disappointing. You would expect climbers to make space round themselves. But in numbers they gather under the same bit of wall, gazing up at the same young star failing on the same 7a problem. They whisper:

"He won't crack it like that."

"I'm really going to practise this winter," I promised Normal. "I'm going to learn to dance."

Normal didn't hear.

"This mad fucker's looking for the one sequence that links all sports centres," he was explaining to someone. "It's common to them all, and if you do it you can travel from one to the other without getting a bus."

I didn't see if Stox found the sequence. He and Normal soon

joined a group of locals working on a figure-four twenty feet above the crash-mats, and I was too shy to have a go. In a figure-four move, you try and sit on your own arm to extend your reach. I finished early. In the entrance hall at Rothwell there are some miserable-looking plants in pots; and, under the broad open staircase, a shallow rectangular pool with goldfish. Coins shine up through the water: the fish nose unexpectantly at them. Bone tired, I hung over the pool while I waited for Normal and Stox to get changed.

"Who would want to throw money in *here*?"

"These Star Bars are excellent, but they don't half clog you up!"

Normal's wife telephoned me.

"We haven't seen you for such a long time," she said. "Hello?"

The call was to invite me to Christmas dinner. Stox would be coming too, she thought. "We'll have all kinds here for the afternoon. We always do!" It was open house as far as she was concerned, just so long as Normal gave her fair warning. But Stox was definitely going on somewhere else in the evening.

"One of the parties in Buxton!" she guessed. "A cavers' party: you know what that means!"

Normal had been a caver for a while, in the mid-to-late Seventies, when it was still possible to be good across the board at "adventure" sports. Distinctions weren't so clear-cut then; less commitment was necessary. (Now only Boy Scouts and army officers are left between the zones of obsession, high and dry, trudging along under a burden of manful, cheery ineptitude like maroons who haven't yet seen the ship sail off without them.) Cavers, anyway, are proud of their parties, which are predicated on a greater despair than climbers can ever experience, the knowledge that you are going down into the ground the next day, where it is dark and cold and smells like a hole in the road; or on a greater joy, which is that you have come up again.

"Anyway," Normal's wife said, "if you aren't doing anything else, the invitation's always open."

"I don't know," I said. "I —"

"There'll be one of my cakes," she promised hurriedly. "And I thought that instead of just sitting around in the afternoon we could go for a walk round Digley."

When I didn't speak she added:

"You know, the reservoir. Is this a bad line?"

"No, I can hear you quite well," I said. "How's Normal?"

"You know Norman!" she said.

He had taken her car to pieces in the road outside the house again. This time it was the wrong rotor arm.

"*Just* what I needed!"

"I'd love to come," I said in the end.

It was three o'clock in the afternoon. As soon as she had rung off I caught a bus into Huddersfield. Lights were already on in the big old gritstone houses behind their holly trees and laurel hedges, curtains already drawn on warm yellow rooms. From the top deck of the bus the square lawns and strings of fairy lights had the look of a comfortable Christmas, intimate and far away. "I'm trying to enjoy life to the full," said a local girl two or three seats behind me to the boy sitting next to her. She was perhaps sixteen, and had the air of someone repeating a piece of received wisdom. "What happened to me?" She laughed. "That's a good question. I got fed up with education, so I found myself a job." It had been a good season for the shops. At first I couldn't find any Christmas cards; then only Old Masters with cracked glaze over dead pheasants, Brueghels full of greed and bustle. I took what I could get, and filled them out in the Merrie England cafe. That year all the women shoppers on New Street seemed to be dressed in imitation of Margaret Thatcher, Princess Diana or Princess Anne. Against the steamy, pseudo-medieval clutter of the Merrie England, this made them seem old; fey, stupid and shrewd all at once; or bored and stolid, their peasant faces heavy with greed. They had looked quite different the year before as they advised each other, "No dear. I've got some Sweetex you can use if you don't want sugar!" A child banged its cup on the table. Through the windows at the end of the cafe you could see into Woolworth's across the road, where two or three Pakistanis were moving aimlessly about. Later I bought a little intricate basket of paper flowers, then struggled back through the crowds — remembering Nina who had once come back from Christmas shopping with her grandmother shouting, "People and pigeons were every-where!" — and arrived home in time to hear the wife from the farm down the road fetching in the cows:

"Kop kop kop," she cried. "Coom on then! Kop kop kop."

I often heard her calling like this, patient and urgent at the same time. "Come on then love," she would vary her rhetoric, as the animals shambled and slithered towards her through the mud, stopping to groan and stare at one another in slow surmise: "Coom on int' yard!"

Sometimes she was so persuasive I wanted to go myself.

Steeplejacking has only a little in common with climbing for fun. The work is hard and the safety precautions minimal. Jacks could protect themselves — on the continent they are required to by law — but it is easier (and quicker, when you are working against a contract deadline) not to bother; and anyway they have a myth of themselves which precludes this. Fearless at the age of eighteen they find themselves, as the juices and daft appetites of youth dry up, trapped in an increasingly irrelevant and dangerous self-image. They take to drink to keep them reckless, or just to get them up in the mornings; or drift away into other kinds of labouring, where they go sour remembering what demigods they used to be. As an apprentice, Stox had ignored the ladders one day and climbed instead the steel reinforcing bands of a 150-foot incinerator chimney on a waste tip near Birmingham. "It was quicker," he claimed; but really he had done it out of mischief, and a desire to stir up his elders. The other jacks, he said, had been "well surprised"; but generally they would admit to no interest in rock climbing, and seemed unimpressed by his photographs of London Wall and Coventry Street.

Stox phoned me at seven in the morning on Christmas Eve and asked me if I'd like to see what jacking was all about. I'd known him for a fortnight. I was so flattered and surprised I could only answer "Yes."

If this seemed brusque he didn't say so.

"I'll pick you up in half an hour."

He turned up ten minutes later, in a bruised Transit van

belonging to his firm. Inside, it smelled of oil, Swarfega and old polypropylene rope. Stox drove impatiently. He was unforgiving of other drivers. But compared to Normal, whose wild lunges, sudden U-turns and lapses of concentration or memory were legend, he seemed quite safe.

"Ever watch stock car racing? *Well* exciting!"

Stox's contract was at a steelworks near Rotherham. Another team had been in the day before to prepare it for him. His brief was to do a Sonartest and make recommendations. I sat in the Transit for half an hour, reading a three-day-old copy of the *Sun*, while he went from Portakabin to Portakabin looking for the site engineer, a thin Sheffield man who took him by the arm, pointed silently at a smallish stack made of riveted steel cylinders, brick-lined, supported at the base by four vanes so that it looked like an abandoned rocket from some old-fashioned war, and promised, "You'll do nowt wi' that."

It was crawling with rust even at ground level. We found five sixteen-foot wooden ladders in situ, tied on at intervals with steel cable. There was a pulley-block in place.

"Are your ropes always this frayed?" I asked.

Stox smiled distantly, and in the faint but authoritative tones of Harry Dean Stanton in *Repo Man* answered: "Steeplejack always seeks out intense situations. It's part of his code."

"Piss off, Stox."

About sixty feet above the ground was a batten-stage, eight planks and a few bits of scaffolding fixed to the stack with cleats, through which it was easy enough to see the ground. It was bitterly cold up there. In winter, climbers try to pick a sheltered crag: here, with three hundred and sixty degrees of air around us, there was nothing between us and the wind. "I couldn't work up here," I said, looking out over British Steel. The skin at the back of my neck crawled. "Not for money. What do you want me to do?"

"You can admire the view."

Parts of the works were being demolished prior to privatisation. For as far as I could see, cutting torches fizzed and flared and sent up showers of sparks from among the buckled girders. Heaps of waste smouldered in the mud between the huge corrugated sheds, giving off an acrid, low-lying smoke through which I could make out gantries crawling with oxygen pipes; muddy yards where the Mercedes, Volvo and Magirus Deutz trucks were parked in rows; the venous curves of a disused railway line — a bright, almost luminous green moss grew between its dull rails. As we walked past the shed now directly below us, I had seen what I thought were huge steel wheels piled on top of one another. They were already beginning to rust. This reminded me of how, at the turn of the eighteenth century, stone from France became cheaper than Hathersage grit. The grindstone industry collapsed, and work stopped in a day. Half-finished millstones are still scattered around at the base of the Peak District edges, for tourists to eat their lunch off.

After a moment or two, a man strolled into view through the smoke, pushed his goggles up on to his forehead, and pissed against the side of a huge tank of brownish liquid.

"Very nice," said Stox.

He held the Sonartest against his ear and shook it.

"This thing's a bit Mickey Mouse today. You're supposed to be able to calibrate it against the samples. Still, it'll have to do."

There was about twenty feet of the stack left above us. Stox smeared some vaseline over the Sonartest pick-up and set off from the batten-stage, ignoring the ladders in a display of pure technical cheek, climbing on bolt-heads, rivets, things I couldn't see, moving up and down with an intent grace while he passed the pick-up over the surface like a doctor's stethoscope and called down the thicknesses — "2.98 . . . 3.77 . . . There's supposed to be four millimetres even, up here . . . 2.01! Site engineer's not daft . . . 3.12 . . . 1.80! . . ." The pick-up left little green patches of Vaseline wherever it went. Brittle flakes showered down on me as Stox scraped the rust away to get a better contact. "Wait a minute," he told himself, "if you —" He swung out lazily and delicately in that characteristic posture of a climber assessing the next few feet, legs straight, heels down, head tilted up intelligently. "Got it. 2.88." By the time he'd finished we were both freezing.

"Time for some nosh," said Stox.

As I was about to leave the batten-stage he stood in my way and stared at me intently. "I land the soft jobs," he said, "the jobs like this, because I got a CSE. Do you see?" His nose was running heavily, his hands and face had gone a pinkish-purple colour. Along with his cropped hair and the two short vertical lines of concentration between his eyebrows, this gave him a raw, hard look. "Most steeplejacks can't find their arses in the morning." For a moment he seemed more disgusted with himself than with them. Then he grinned. "So it's time for some nosh now," he said, letting me on to the ladder. "And that's another hundred quid in the bank. Eh?"

Rotherham might have been abandoned for all we could tell, like the steelworks. Housing estates of a kind of lugubrious maroon brick peered down through clouds of tarry orange smoke on to British Steel: acres of rubble, blowing waste paper, bulldozers. Dogs ran about on the bleak muddy expanses of grass in front of the houses. All the cafes were closed. In the end we went into a pub, where Stox bought a plate of pork pies, a whisky-and-Coke. "Look at that," he congratulated himself. He sat down and opened a recent issue of *Stock Car Monthly*.

"The reason I like stockers so much," he said, "is the *start*. You've never seen anything like it for sheer violence. Really."

He leaned forward over the table.

"Ever been? One minute nothing's happening. They're just cruising round the pace lap. The next it's like *Apocalypse Now* in a cinema full of hot dog stands. You can't see for cinders and all you can smell is fried onions. Fucking awesome! You get used to it after a lap though, so I just go for the starts. Did you see that film? *Apocalypse Now*? Brilliant!"

He finished the pork pies. He wiped his mouth and said with a grin:

"And what's this I hear about you screwing Normal's wife?"

I only ever went over to Morecambe once. It was late in the day when we got there, but the sky was like brass. I remember the placid muddy water of the boating pool, beyond which rotting piles go out into some great slow tidal stream slipping past to join the Kent Channel; sleeping women on the sand, their dresses pulled up to expose their legs to the thick hot light; the giant cone above the ice cream stall. In a fish restaurant they advertised "best butter" on the bread. A man finished his meal then stared ahead with his mouth open while two teenage couples took photographs of each other across the table with a cheap camera. Music hung in the air in the amusement park, with diesel smoke and the smell of fried fish: "Blue Moon, now I'm no longer alone." A dog trotted by. Nobody was playing at the Catch-a-Duck stall.

I felt relaxed and elated, both at once. The music, the signs on the sea front, the thick horizontal evening light which seemed to slip over us like warm water, might all have been one thing, one stimulus or substance appealing to a single simple sensory organ we all used to have but now forget we possess.

Later, at the hotel, Normal's wife knelt on the edge of the bed, leaning forward supported by her elbows. She had pulled her pleated Marks & Spencers skirt up around her waist. Her elevated thighs were bare; between them, the white gusset of her knickers contained her sex, shaping it into a clean plump cotton purse. Suddenly she moved her knees apart so that I could see her round shiny face upside down between her legs. Complexion reddening, body swaying just slightly with the effort, she looked like a big child with a new enthusiasm; or a Polaroid from *Fiesta*'s "Readers' Wives" in 1979, in which the very ungainliness and naivety of the exhibitionism caught at your throat with a mixture of compassion and greed.

"Aren't we going to do anything?" she said.

"In a minute, Margaret."

For two hours a thunderstorm had been moving furtively along the horizon. I couldn't tell whether it was inland, fumbling its way over the quarries east and south of Preston, separating them briefly with its fingers of rain and darkness, looking in, pushing them away; or somewhere out to sea like a great wheel of light.

Margaret allowed herself to fall sideways on to the bed.

"Did you see those women on the beach? Honestly!"

She rearranged her skirt.

"When I was eight," she said, "I ran into a disused electrical socket in the lounge."

As a result of this three stitches had to be put in her forehead: "He was such a sweet old doctor. 'Now I'm going to do this without an anaesthetic,' he told my father, 'but you mustn't think it's because I'm being cruel. It's in case there are problems later.' Daddy didn't know what he meant."

She gave me a wide smile and pulled back her hair. "But he was quite right. Look! No scar!"

Perhaps a month had passed since I first spoke to her for any length of time, in the yeasty heat of Normal's front room, then in his rock garden. I order my memories of that afternoon in time to the breathing sound of a saw. Off at the edge of the estate, dogs barked, children called to one another. Wasps buzzed past us in long determined arcs, attracted by the mess Normal had made in the kitchen. She had come down the garden, you remember, to find me. "I see you're admiring the quarry. I call it his quarry." She had washed her face carefully. The black velvet pansy was pinned to her blouse. About to speak, she turned her head — in the next house they had switched a radio on, then after some argument off again.

"Your hair's very nice today," she said eventually. "Have you just had it cut?"

I stared at her.

"Norman can't help the way he is."

Which of us said that? What mattered at the time, I suppose, was that neither of us believed it; or cared. Somehow, in trying to say something about the black pansy, or touch it, I touched Margaret instead, and was shocked by the suddenness and certainty of her response. "Let's go inside! Let's go inside!" We lay on the front room carpet in a bar of sunlight, looking at one another, smiling and shivering with nerves. I kicked my rucksack out of the way. The flowers on their glass shelves had a scent now. We had known this — whatever it was — about one another since I walked into the house. "Here!" "I love you." The warmth when I entered her was such a shock I thought I had come; it was like a ripple going across a familiar landscape — everything is what it was before, everything is different, everything is what it was before — a heat-shimmer on a summer day.

"There! There! You see?"

"Oh."

In the hotel room at Morecambe, perhaps, these certainties had already begun to seem less clear. Sankey was dead and buried. A fly looped repetitively across the blank television screen in the corner, its shadow preceding it. "I adore hotel rooms," said Margaret. She pushed the window up, leaned far out, and looked across the town towards the funfair, the distant sea. I remembered Normal telling me about Ed, who had earned his living here as a photographer, and I wondered if through her own Morecambe she could see any of Ed's: and then, transposed very faintly upon that, any of his South America of the mind.

"It's best to get sex over with as quickly as possible in weather like this," she said. "Not that you don't enjoy it. But if you aren't quick you can get sticky."

"It didn't last long," I told Stox. "Normal doesn't know."

Stox grinned.

"I never said he did."

He emptied his glass.

"That's whisky-and-Coke," he prompted me, pushing it over the table. "You tight bastard."

20 · ROCK GARDENS

This summer I photographed two cormorants standing on the edge of Porthmoina Island, Bosigran, West Penwith. Just after I pressed the shutter, they dived suddenly into the water.

At Bosigran the cliff goes up blinding white in the sun. From a distance, the glossy ivy on the boulders underneath gives it the air of a wall round a prosperous Penwith garden. After I had photographed the cormorants I put my magic boots on and climbed up the first two pitches of a route called Doorpost. This brought me out on to comfortable ledges in a sunny niche a hundred and fifty feet up, from which I could look out over Porthmoina cove at the sea boiling round the wet black aprons of granite at the base of Commando Ridge. From that height, the sea has a surface resembling intensely-rippled glass. It takes faith to penetrate the world the way a cormorant must. If I were one I would have to promise myself every day, "The water looks impervious: but at the right moment it will give." I sat in the niche for a long time. I realised I didn't know any more than I had the last time I sat there. I didn't know anything about anything.

It was late evening when I climbed out, dark as I walked back up the path to the car-park.

The Polaroids I took the year Sankey died have developed with age. They tended to be over-exposed, but details previously awash in light can now be discerned quite clearly:

Bamburgh Castle has formed itself out of the morning haze and, seen in the distance behind the bonnet of Sankey's Reliant, presents an exact if romantic outline of towers and stepped walls where originally it was hardly visible. The awning of the Hot Snax van in the lay-by at Kirkby Lonsdale on the A65 has begun at last to show mint-green stripes originally bleached by the six a.m. August sunshine into a white blur; a middle-aged woman in a print frock — caught in her moment of indecision, tea or coffee? — stands before it. As if pigments could learn about what they represent, events understand themselves more accurately towards the end than the beginning, the freshly quarried boulders photographed at Millstone Edge have confirmed their outlines and no longer resemble melted lumps of sugar.

This clarification has gone further in some shots than in others. In the blurred Polaroid I tried to show Sankey's sister, for example, the climber could still be any of us, crabbing his way across the concrete of the Richard Dunn wall — which at that point is seamed with shallow, sharp-edged cracks, lipped enough for your fingers only where you don't need it — just in advance of some small ongoing disaster, some failure of logic in the world itself. A snap even less communicative shows Mick from the pipeworks: unreconstructed and paranoid-looking — to the extent that you can see him at all — he stands on one of the Cromlech boulders, leering sideways at the camera through a grey leached-out air, his head tilted back as if to howl or crow. For some reason he is wearing his pullover as a pair of trousers.

Lovers, tribesmen and lunatics:

Gaz grins awkwardly up from a move on Wildcat Tor, his face gaining colour as it curdles year by year out of the glare of the built-in flash; the photographer's foot can be seen in the left-hand bottom corner, and the ledge Gaz is making for is covered in fallen leaves. (In another picture, his wife has put her arms affectionately round his waist from behind and now rubs her face on his shoulder. At their feet the baby, in its red pants and grubby white T-shirt, sits on the hard-packed earth underneath Wall of Bubbles at Stoney, eating rock-boot laces to improve its technique.) Bob Almanac stares speculatively at the tangled mass of tapes, rope and wired runners he has just pulled out of his rucksack, like some shopper holding up a dead chicken by the neck. Normal, using my camera, has caught Sankey and me on a beach somewhere, washing an aluminium pan; the sun blazes off it into our eyes, making us seem puzzled and diffident. Here's Mick again, fishing with a tin mug fifteen hundred feet up in the Langdales, reflected precisely in the water of Stickle Tarn. "I've got eight here!" I remember him shouting to us. "Eight of the little fuckers!" In the photo his mouth is a perfect O of delight.

I remember a blazing day we had in August or September on the Pembroke sea cliffs. As soon as you got down to the sea-level platform at Stennis Head, you were transfixed: the rock yawned up, acres of blinding white limestone in the sun, less like an amphitheatre than a vast parabolic mirror, with you at its exact centre of focus. At any moment, you felt, you might be ignited, fired up like a carbon arc: you might be converted into pure light. There's a Polaroid of this too. I don't know who took it, because all the climbers are in it, grinning, eyes screwed up against the sun: Gaz and Sankey, Bob and David, Mick and his girlfriend, Normal and me. The route we have just ticked, Welcome to the Pleasure Dome, arches triumphally up behind us, the best climb any of us did all year. Our T-shirts are fastened on to our heads with bits of coloured nylon line, to fall back over our reddened shoulders like Arab headdresses. Mick's girlfriend has crooked her arm to show her muscles.